Ready for Sea!

Ready for Sea!

How to Outfit the Modern Cruising Sailboat
and Prepare Your Vessel and Yourself
for Extended Passage-Making and Living Aboard

TOR PINNEY

Illustrations by Bruce Bingham

SHERIDAN HOUSE

First published 2002 by
Sheridan House Inc.
145 Palisade Street
Dobbs Ferry, NY 10522
www.sheridanhouse.com

Library of Congress Cataloging-in-Publication Data

Pinney, Tor.
  Ready for sea!: how to outfit the modern cruising sailboat
  and prepare your vessel for extended passage-making
  and living aboard/Tor Pinney; illustrations by Bruce Bingham.
      p.cm
  Includes index.
  ISBN 1-57409-144-1 (alk. paper)
  1. Sailing—Handbooks, manuals, etc. 2. Sailboats—
  Handbooks, manuals, etc. I. Title.

  GV811. P57 2002
  797.1'24—dc21   2001057641

Edited by Ray Jason
Managing editor: Janine Simon
Designed by Keata Brewer
Illustrations by Bruce Bingham, except for Figures 15a, b, c and d
Figure 9 reprinted by permission of The McGraw-Hill Companies

Printed in the United States of America

ISBN   1-57409-144-1

*The love that is given to ships is profoundly different
from the love men feel for every other work of their hands.*
Joseph Conrad

Everything can be found at sea according to the spirit of your quest.
Joseph Conrad

Contents

‿⌒

Have Fun; Plan Ahead; Be Safe; Manual Back-ups;
Double-Functions; Integrated Systems;
Money; Choosing the Boat; Go!

Basic Equipment List

The Masthead; The Mast; Standing Rigging;
Backstay; Running and Intermediate Backstays;
Inner Forestay Quick Release Lever; Running Rigging;
Keel-Stepped, Deck-Stepped and Tabernacle Masts;
Mast Pulpits, Lines Led Aft and Reefing Systems;
Mast Ladder Steps; Roller Furling/Reefing;
Whisker Poles and Twin Headsails; Lazy Jacks;
Flags; Deck Lights; Tri-Color Masthead Light;
Strobe Lights; Radar Reflector; Lightning Ground

Sails; Tell-tales; Canvas Accessories;
Drogues, Sea Anchors and Warps

Acknowledgments

No author is an island. I've learned so much of what I know from others that it hardly seems fair for me to get the credit just because I put it down on paper. First of all, I thank Mother Ocean, who teaches tirelessly and without prejudice. I thank the sailboats I've owned (and which, at the time, owned me): KONA, THUMPER, BLUE BALLS, AUTANT, BUCCANEER, KERRY, SPARROW, and ADAGIO.

Thank you Ray Jason—sailor, writer, friend and editor of this book.

I owe a debt of gratitude to Captain Ron Trossbach, former Director of Navy Sailing, for his knowledgeable contributions to this text. Miami-based specialists who generously shared their expertise include master rigger Gary Shotwell of Sailing Services Grove, Inc., and engineer Red Conklin of Shipwreck Services, Inc. Electrical engineer Rod Dimich (s/v GOLIARD) designed and installed SPARROW's integrated energy system. Thanks Rod, it worked.

Thank you, Henry Mohrschladt and Mike Howarth, founders of Pacific Seacraft, for having faith in me, giving me a chance to earn and customize my dream boat, and then building it for me. Thanks to Rich Worstell, president of Valiant Yachts, for showing me years later how to build a perfect offshore cruising sailboat.

Thanks especially to Sherrie Kisiel Jans for years of advice and encouragement, and to John C. Nelson, Paul Gilling, Andrea Arel, Roy Pinney, Debbie Liu Gillette, and Ralph Perrson for their editorial assistance. Thanks to my daughter, Lisa, and my two salty dogs, Shaolin and La Rosa Española de Sevilla, for patiently letting me write when they really wanted to go ashore.

Special thanks to Jack Hedden, a true yachtsman, who was my mentor and friend when I was learning to sail, and to the others—too many to name—who aided and abetted.

All of the above notwithstanding, responsibility for the content of this book rests solely with the author.

Preface

⌣⌐

This book is about outfitting today's cruising sailboat for long-distance voyaging and long-term living aboard. In it we'll consider equipment, systems and modifications that will transform a basic sail-away boat— one already operational and of sound construction—into a long-range cruiser thoroughly prepared to carry a liveaboard crew across oceans and to visit distant shores. Even if the cruising is limited to short vacation excursions, every captain strives to do all he can to prepare himself and his ship for any eventuality. Our goal, then, is to be self sufficient, through good planning, while we cruise. This book also provides valuable outfitting checklists, which I believe to be the most thorough of their kind, to which you can refer and add.

The number of subjects, skills and sciences that have a direct bearing on cruising is almost limitless. Topics such as yacht design, construction and purchase apply before outfitting, while others like route planning, maintenance and sailing techniques come afterwards. Although I occasionally touch on these "before and after" subjects while discussing equipment and systems, the intent of *Ready for Sea!* is to bridge the gap in between, ensuring that the boat you own will fulfill her maximum potential as a world voyager.

Taken separately, nearly every single subject covered in the following pages could be expanded to fill an entire book all by itself. Indeed, I'd venture to say most of them have been. There simply is not room in any one book to discuss every one of these topics in complete detail. I encourage you to seek additional information on the subjects that interest you by attending boat shows, by reading other, subject-specific books and magazine articles, and by talking with sailors and technical experts. What I hope to accomplish in this book is simply to make you aware of the many possibilities when outfitting a sailboat for cruising, to point you in the right direction.

My most recent (fifth) cruising sailboat, christened SPARROW, was an American-built Pacific Seacraft Crealock 37. SPARROW was the prototype of a special series of Pacific Seacraft boats called Circum-navigators. These featured a factory options package that I designed for the builder, all of which (and much more) is discussed in this book. Nevertheless, the ideas herein apply to virtually all cruising sailboats, regardless of origin and size.

I hope this information adds to the safety and pleasure of the cruising life for my fellow sailors. If so, the effort of writing it down will have been worthwhile.

Ready for Sea!

Introduction

⌒⌐

How I Came to the Sea— From Rock-and-Roll to Rocking and Rolling

When I was a teenager, I was invited to go for a daysail aboard a family friend's yacht, a 35-foot sloop, on Long Island Sound. The sail was exhilarating! A stiff breeze and a white-capped chop brought the little ship to life. But what really impressed me, what absolutely electrified my young imagination the more I recognized its implications, was what I discovered belowdecks. I had never before seen the inside of a proper yacht that size. "This is incredible," I thought, "there's a kitchen, a desk and a dining table, a bathroom, beds, books . . . *Why, you could actually live on one of these, and travel!*"

That was the beginning of the end. I was so moved by the experience that I soon became hopelessly obsessed with the idea, the lifestyle, the freedom and pure joy of liveaboard cruising. *Ready for Sea!* summarizes much of what I've learned about outfitting a sailboat in the decades since that epiphany.

That I was drawn to a life of travel, adventure, boats and the sea isn't so surprising. My mother, a famous baby photographer and now an artist, crewed for years in sailboat races on Long Island Sound. My father, a naturalist and herpetologist with two-dozen books and many documentary films to his credit, has traveled to the world's most remote regions for the better part of a century, sometimes taking me with him. My Norwegian grandfather, Arndt Bertelsen, was the son of a boatbuilder, from a long line of seamen dating back to the Vikings. He shipped out of Oslo on a three-masted barque in 1914, survived a torpedo sinking in the North Sea during World War I, and went on to skipper ships from the Arctic to West Africa before he settled in America and became an engineer at the Brooklyn Navy Yard. My paternal family name is Schiffer, which literally means boatman or skipper. My brother, Roy, sells yachts in Fort Lauderdale. Two of my best friends, Paul Gilling and John Nelson, are also yacht brokers and the rest are cruising sailors, or ought to be. I guess you could say travel, adventure, boats and the sea are in my blood.

My path to the sea, however, was a tortuous one at first. I was sidetracked by the needs, interests and problems of an adolescent becoming a young man. Besides, it was hard to realize that such a thing was really even possible. Living on a sailboat was unheard of in the 1960s, at least in Larchmont, New York, where I grew up. With the exception of a handful of voyagers then unknown to me, such as Eric and Susan Hiscock, Hal and Margaret Roth, and of course the founding father of it all, Joshua Slocum, people did not even think about what today is commonly called liveaboard cruising. Oh, yachtsmen made voyages, to be sure, but then they went home. As far as I knew, people didn't actually *live* on boats.

During the next couple of years, the dream of setting sail gradually grew into a burning desire. I finished high school and went to Syracuse University, as I was expected to do. But college bored me— the subjects were lifeless and the gray, wet weather depressing—and so my real life began when I dropped out after only one semester, stepped onto a southbound Interstate, and stuck out my thumb. From that moment on, I was on my own and headed for the sea. Eventually.

Within the year, I married my high school sweetheart and soon became a young father. Alas, the marriage was not to last, but my relationship with my daughter did. To this day Lisa is the light of my life. She has been sailing with me many times, all over the world. Recently, she made me a (young) grandfather and if I have anything to do with it, little Reece, like his mother before him, will learn to sail a boat way before he learns to drive a car. But I was talking about how I came to the sea.

I had been playing in rock'n'roll bands since junior high school, and was a tolerable guitar player, singer and songwriter. Needing a way to support my new family, I put together a rock group and we were soon performing in New York City's hip nightclubs. My hair was getting long and as Bob Dylan sang, the times they were a changin'. I was at the heart of the new hippie scene and experimenting with everything. It got pretty wild—a little too wild—and it was becoming evident to me that I had better distance myself from it a bit. Right about then my brother invited me to take over a rock band he had put together in Texas. I jumped at the opportunity and into my old, convertible Corvair and headed west.

The group, called the Chains, was a big fish in a small pond, enjoying a string of regional hit records in the western states. I had actually written a couple of the songs they recorded. For the next year and a half, we played dances and rock shows from Texas to Montana, dodging the truck stop rednecks who thought hippies were fair game, feeling like stars, and generally having a pretty good time until the promise of a big-time recording contract lured us all back to New York City.

The contract never materialized and I lost interest in playing in nightclubs. So I left the Chains to try my hand at Madison Avenue jingle writing. To keep me from starving meanwhile, my manager landed me a part-time job giving guitar lessons to actor Dustin Hoffman three times a week in his Upper East Side apartment, preparing him for a scene in a movie he was making that required him to strum three cords and look natural about it. Dustin was a nice guy and I liked him, but he wasn't really into learning guitar. He never practiced except during the thrice-weekly, one-hour sessions with me. For this reason he learned slowly, which was great for me because I needed the $12 an hour his movie production company paid me.

I wasn't having much luck as an advertising jingle writer and, when Dustin went off to make his movie, I needed a new gig. Just then, my manager called me with a proposition. "Tor," he said, "you know that new record on the radio called 'Na Na Hey Hey Kiss 'Em

Goodbye'?" Well, of course I did. It was a huge, number one smash hit all over the United States and around the world. To this day, kids still chant the chorus at school football games. He went on to explain that the record had been a studio creation and that there was really no such group as Steam, the band credited with the recording. Now that the record had taken off, the producer was being bombarded with requests for the non-existent stars to perform at concerts, college homecomings and rock festivals coast to coast, and was actually booking the band's first national tour. They desperately needed a group that could perform that song convincingly along with enough other material for a 45-minute show, and my manager was offering me the job of putting that band together.

The tour sounded like a blast and the money was good, so ten days later my new quartet went on tour as Steam. We Na–Na–Hey–Hey'ed our way all across the country, signing autographs, dodging the red-necks and loving the groupies. It was the beginning of the '70s in all its glory and, man, we were cool. Most of my old school chums were either still in college or trying to stay alive in Vietnam.

After a year or so of being a bubblegum rock star, I sold a song I'd written to Columbia Records and spent the advance money on a plane ticket to Morocco. For the next couple of months, I hitchhiked through Europe, lived in a commune on the island of Mallorca with author Robert Graves for a neighbor, and finished up in the smoky coffee houses of Amsterdam. I still couldn't afford a boat, but life was good.

All the time I was in show business, my desire to live and travel aboard my own sailboat grew steadily stronger until it became an ob-session. I read books about it. I fantasized about it. Every new gig, every recording contract was supposed to be my ticket to freedom, my pot of gold. It never quite turned out that way, but I was determined to keep trying.

Next came a stint as a rock'n'roll songwriter, under contract with an Atlanta-based record company. They actually paid me a retainer and put me up in a swanky garden apartment in Buckhead. My job was to hang out and write songs, let my hair grow even longer, smoke and party all night long, write more songs, sleep late, flirt with the stewardesses and nurses that lived in my apartment complex and go into a big, state-of-the-art recording studio a few times a week to tape demo sessions and oversee the arrangements whenever their other bands recorded my material. I was in hog heaven, as those good old Atlanta boys would say—until their record company went belly-up and I found myself on the street again.

I heard of try-outs being held for something they were calling a "rock opera." I didn't want to go back to playing in bands again, so I went to the audition. It turned out that my hard-rock stage experience and gutsy vocal style was just what they wanted for the lead role, and so I became Judas in the rock opera, *Jesus Christ Superstar*, the Atlanta production. The show was an instant and, in the South of the early 1970s, controversial hit and we were packing the theater in Underground Atlanta, 14 shows a week. One evening, the governor of Georgia showed up in the audience to check out our show. Afterwards, he came backstage with his wife and bodyguards to meet the cast and get us to autograph his libretto. I addressed my signature to *JC Super Governor*, the "JC" standing, of course, for Jimmy Carter.

Having seen how *Jesus Christ Superstar*'s producers had put that show together, I decided I could be a producer, too. I found a financial backer in Atlanta, flew to New York, met with the U.S. managers of the superstar rock band, the Who, and got exclusive stage performance rights for the Southeastern United States for their rock opera, *Tommy*.

My rendition of *Tommy* was a colorful, multi-media stage production featuring a troop of modern dancers, a black African choreographer, a professional director, special effects stage lighting and a live band that blasted out those songs better than the original soundtrack. Producing a show like that turned out to be more involved than I had anticipated, and I worked myself into a state of exhaustion molding that company of 30 creative talents into a single performing unit. The show opened on time, went on the road and got standing ovations for every performance it did for the next two years. For my part, I was burned out by opening night. Besides, the mechanics of managing the road tour didn't interest me, so I left the company to my successors.

The truth was, the urge to be on a sailboat headed for some tropical island was burning in me with a passion and all else seemed lukewarm by comparison. So at long last, ready or not, I packed my meager belongings into an old pickup truck and headed for the coast.

I wound up in Wrightsville Beach, North Carolina, where I found a job in a boatyard for minimum wage. I wanted to learn everything I could about boats, from the bottom up, and that's exactly what the yard manager had in mind. He put me to work scraping and painting the bottoms of boats that hauled out there. Gradually, I learned to paint hulls, install equipment, use bedding compounds, do simple engine and rigging repairs, and so on. I was no closer to affording a sailboat than I had been when I was 16, but I was happy to be within sight of the ocean at long last.

Halfway through that summer, a couple of ex-GI's pulled into the marina aboard a 40-foot ketch, on their way to the Islands. One evening we were sharing a six-pack in their cockpit and the skipper said I'd be welcome to come along as crew if I wanted to. He did not have to say it twice. Within the week I sold my truck, quit my job, moved aboard, and put to sea. In a sense, I've never come back.

For the next couple of years, I crewed on a host of different boats, ranging as far as the West Indies and South America. Every voyage was an adventure, every passage a teacher. The captains and mates I sailed with, the weather we braved, the ports we made and the lessons learned in those first years could fill a book, and maybe they will someday.

At last, in the spring of 1974, my dream finally came true. I bought a sailboat and moved aboard. Then came the day of days, a bright morning full of promise, with a breeze just fair enough for a single, sweeping tack down Biscayne Bay. I weighed anchor, slipped quietly out of the Coconut Grove anchorage and headed down the Florida Keys. Long-haired, bearded, 20-something, practically penniless and perfectly content, I set off on my first singlehanded voyage aboard my first liveaboard sailboat.

She was no ordinary sailboat, either. THUMPER was a converted lifeboat, salvaged by my predecessor from an old World War II Liberty ship being scrapped in the Chesapeake. She was a salty old dog and the queen of my heart, though you might not have called her graceful. A tubby 24-footer, eight feet wide almost her entire length and double-

THUMPER was my first liveaboard cruising sailboat. Not big, not fancy, but she was mine and I've never loved a boat more *(Marty Mullin)*

ended only at the last possible moment, THUMPER had been built in another era and for another purpose. She was made of riveted steel plates and sported a stout spruce mast held aloft by cables, deadeyes and lanyards, flying a gaff-rigged mainsail and a sadly worn working jib. With no electrical system, her running lights were kerosene and her one massive bilge pump, manual. She was mostly an open boat, but with an added-on plywood cuddy cabin forward, just big enough for a cozy couple to sleep. Original oak plank lifeboat benches ran around the inside of the hull and amidships squatted a husky Gray Marine gasoline engine, held together with Marine Tex and bailing wire and started by means of a heavy iron hand-crank—like an old Model T automobile. I paid $1,000 for her.

When I sold THUMPER about a year later, I found my way to Maui and liked it enough to stay for a while, playing folk music at a tourist bar for my living money. When it was time to go, I had just enough

My second cruising boat, the 50-year-old, gaff-rigged ketch AUTANT was a classic beauty with no electronics and no engine. *(Doris Pinney Brenner)*

for a plane ticket to Los Angeles and had to hitchhike the rest of the way back to Coconut Grove, Florida.

In America, an entrepreneur doesn't have to stay broke for long. I designed and produced a line of jewelry, then a line of tropical clothing, and before long I had scraped up enough money to buy the ketch AUTANT, a classic beauty I found forlorn and for sale on the Miami River. Designed by William Hand and built in 1927 of double diagonal strip-planking, her hull was over 2" thick and very strong. Her stout gaff main and mizzen and self-tending jib allowed for fairly easy handling by a lone sailor, which was just as well because AUTANT had no engine in her. She also had no electrical system, no plumbing, no winches, or other modern conveniences. She was all kerosene lamps, block-and-tackle, and muscle. A simple sailboat with character, she measured 36 feet on deck; about 42 feet overall. I lived aboard and cruised the Florida Keys and the Bahamas with her for two and a half years.

I turned 29 singlehanding AUTANT back from the Abacos. Realizing I would soon be attaining the ancient age of 30, I decided it was time to upgrade my life, find a way to voyage farther on finer boats, and get paid for it. So when I got back to Miami, I took a crash course and passed the Coast Guard exam for my 100-ton license. I had some business cards printed up that said Captain Tor Pinney, typed up a resume, and commenced my life as a professional delivery and charter skipper. For the next few years I alternated between running charter sailboats in the Virgin Islands and delivering yachts between the U.S. East Coast and the West Indies. I sailed almost constantly during that period and logged tens of thousands of nautical miles.

In 1980, I traveled to Costa Rica to backpack around for a month or so. There I met up with a company in San Jose building an unknown, salty-looking fiberglass sailboat they called the Cabo Rico 38. They were hoping to break into the lucrative U.S. marketplace with these boats and needed someone to find stateside dealerships for them. It was agreed that I would do just that, and I spent the next year as Cabo Rico's factory representative, living in motels, rental cars, and a VW pop-top camper van. I traveled coast to coast and eventually signed up six stocking dealers. When it was over I had created Cabo

Rico's first dealership network, and they have done well in the United States ever since.

I had also earned enough in commissions to pay for my next boat, a steel Finisterre yawl named BUCCANEER. For years I had seen her berthed in Coconut Grove's Dinner Key Marina, and now she was for sale. Designed by Sparkman and Stevens and custom built in Chicago in 1959, BUCCANEER had a low freeboard, a broad beam and a sheer line as graceful as a swan. A beautiful sailboat, she was often mistaken for a Bermuda 40.

My new mate and I sailed BUCCANEER up to the Chesapeake Bay and from the beginning, it was difficult to say which of my two girls was the more cantankerous. My mate's troubles are another story altogether, but it turned out BUCCANEER needed a huge amount of hull re-plating, her steel having rusted from the inside way beyond what the surveyor had detected. Lucky for me, I had a friend with a boatyard on the Bohemia River. There we spent an entire summer sandblasting, grinding, re-plating, repairing, replacing and reconditioning the old witch stem to stern. By the time we sailed for the West Indies in early December, there was ice on the decks and precious little left in the cruising kitty.

The next year I was invited to captain the prototype Morgan 60 schooner, PARADIGM, first through a series of East Coast fall boat shows, and then for a season of chartering in the Virgin Islands. Two significant things happened that year: I met, befriended and got drunk with Tristan Jones at a couple of those boat shows, and I rescued a dory-full of commercial fishermen after they had abandoned their burning ship in mid-ocean. Oh, there was one other thing. I convinced Pacific Seacraft to give me a new Crealock 37 sailboat.

Well, maybe give is an exaggeration. I had decided I wanted that boat and so approached the builder with a proposal. I would open their first Southeast U.S. dealership in Fort Lauderdale and promote and sell their boats fulltime if they would send me a demo boat. I promised to pay them for the boat, plus interest, out of the commissions I earned. We struck a bargain and I became a yacht broker and regional dealer for Pacific Seacraft. The brand new demo boat arrived. I named her KERRY and moved aboard. For the next four and a half years, I lived

BUCCANEER was a steel Finisterre yawl, pretty and fast, but surely the most cantankerous boat I ever owned. *(Doris Pinney Brenner)*

dockside except for occasional demo sails, holiday cruises and boat shows, and I worked hard at my new profession. I managed to pay off that boat in the first 18 months.

I had promised myself I would only stay put for five years at the most and I was already planning my escape by 1987. I'd sold quite a few cruising sailboats by that time, new and used, and noticed that more often than not, the buyers had many questions about how to outfit

Pacific Seacraft sent me KERRY as a demo boat. I lived aboard while using her to sell more boats for the builder. *(Paul Gilling)*

their boats to go cruising. Pacific Seacraft built good boats and rightfully touted them as bluewater passagemakers, yet when the new boats came from the factory they were nowhere near ready to actually go cruising. There was no ground tackle, no safety equipment, no spare parts kit, minimal electronics, no awnings, jacklines or self-steering, the floorboards weren't secured for capsize... The list of what needed to be done was enormous. The people buying these boats could generally afford to pay for all the additional stuff, but hardly knew where to begin selecting and assembling it.

So I made a new proposal to Pacific Seacraft. I suggested they offer an upgraded version of their Crealock 37, which was the biggest boat they built at the time. This special edition would feature a long list of equipment and systems added according to my specifications. We'd call it the Crealock 37 "Circumnavigator", and I was volunteering to introduce it at the 1988 East Coast fall boat shows. I also asked them to build the first one for me . . . for a discounted price, since it was my idea. In return, I would design the equipment and systems package that became the Circumnavigator, write the copy for their advertisements, and arrange to take the prototype to all the boat shows as a factory rep, allowing the other regional dealers to sell from my demo boat. Pacific Seacraft thought it was a worthwhile idea and agreed to the plan.

My brand new Circumnavigator arrived Christmas week 1987. I christened her SPARROW after the famous calypso singer/songwriter, the Mighty Sparrow. For the next few months, I worked with a crew installing equipment and modifying or inventing systems to make her into my idea of the perfect liveaboard cruising sailboat. Afterwards, when I took her to the boat shows, a lot of people seemed to agree that I'd gotten it right. That Circumnavigator package was the seed from which this book eventually grew.

And so it was that by the end of my five-year stint as a yacht broker/dealer, I had put my daughter through college, socked away a cruising kitty, fulfilled my obligations to Pacific Seacraft, owned an extraordinarily well-found sailboat, and had the freedom, the ability and the time to take her anywhere in the world. Life was good, even though I turned 40.

SPARROW was my penultimate cruising sailboat, well-outfitted for world voyaging. She carried me safely over 30,000 nautical miles during our six-year adventure. *(Tor Pinney)*

SPARROW carried me safely over 30,000 nautical miles during the next six years. Half the time I singlehanded, more by circumstance than by choice. The other half of the time, my crew consisted of, at first, my fiancée, Sherrie, and our 90-lb. yellow Labrador, Shaolin, and then later, after they abandoned ship and moved to Alaska, my new love, Andrea, and my new dog, La Rosa Española de Sevilla (Rosa for short), and in between times an assortment of family, friends, and others I met along the way. We sailed from Miami to Maine and back, then to Venezuela via the West Indies. We cruised extensively through Los Roques, Curaçao, Honduras, Guatemala, and Belize and back to Florida. Next came a trans-Atlantic via Beaufort, Bermuda and the Azores to Lisbon, and on to Spain where we wintered in Seville and Cádiz. Gibraltar followed, then the Balearics, Sardinia, Sicily, the Greek Islands and Turkey. Finally, we backtracked through the Mediterranean by way of Tunisia and Gibraltar, fought our way to the Canary Islands, re-crossed the Atlantic to Grenada, and ambled up through the West Indies to Puerto Rico, the Bahamas and finally back to Florida, where I sold SPARROW. I wrote much of this book during that cruise, benefiting from the opportunity to find out first hand what equipment and systems really worked and what didn't, both on my own boat and on many others I studied.

For my next venture, I bought a 65-foot, 175-passenger ferry boat in Ontario, Canada, hired a crane to plunk a slide-on camper unit onto the upper deck to serve as temporary living quarters, and drove that unlikely-looking vessel 2,000 miles by way of the Great Lakes, the Erie Canal, the Hudson River and the Intracoastal Waterway to Key West, Florida, where I ran her as a riotous tourist excursion boat for a few years. On the upper deck, my partner and I installed a giant Jacuzzi, a real sand beach, live palm trees in planters, and tables and chairs, all surrounded by a tiki thatch skirt around the railing. On the main deck, indoors, was a full liquor bar specializing in frozen tropical drinks, a snack stand, restrooms, more tables and chairs, and a dance floor with live reggae music and limbo dancing. The bulkheads were adorned with hand-painted tropical murals and the entire ship was one big island party. Am I crazy? You tell me. It was a wild ride.

When I left Key West, I went cruising again, but this time in a 23-foot RV with Rosa, a little 12-pound mutt I had rescued from starving

I converted RUMRUNNER KEY from a Canadian ferry boat into a wacky tourist party boat and operated her in Key West, Florida, for a few years. *(Tor Pinney)*

I earned a USCG 100-ton license and started getting paid to deliver sailboats to the West Indies. *(Doris Pinney Brenner)*

on the streets of Seville back when I'd been there aboard SPARROW. I wanted to see more of the United States inland, so for the next couple of years, we roamed around out west, through the Grand Canyon and the Rocky Mountains, eventually settling for a year in Mount Shasta, just south of the Oregon border. I camped, hiked, trail-biked, white-water-rafted, kayaked, climbed, skied and snow-shoed all over the Rockies and the Cascades and I have to admit I grew to love the wild mountain forests as much as I love the ocean. I hope to share my time between the two in the future.

As of this writing, I'm back to selling boats, this time in Rhode Island, halfway through another five-year plan. I'm a worldwide dealer for Valiant Yachts semi-custom cruising sailboats and Nova Scotia-built Cape Island trawlers these days, and an Internet-focused yacht broker for all kinds of other used cruising sailboats all over the world. It's good to make a living helping sailors find and sell their dreamboats. I believe that you can get everything in this world that you want if you just help enough other people get what they want.

So, what's next? Who knows? Another boat, for sure, and maybe a slow poke through the South Pacific and the Indian Ocean, alternating with some more RV time in the Northwest and Canadian mountains and some rucksack traveling in Asia and Africa. So many places, so little time. Life is good.

Just as I wrote songs in my rock'n'roll years, I eventually started writing stories and articles, mostly for boating magazines, when I took to the sea. After a while, it seemed natural to write something longer. The many boats I've outfitted for cruising and for offshore deliveries, and the years I spent helping my customers, Pacific Seacraft and Valiant Yachts, outfit their cruising sailboats, together gave birth to this book. It's most of what I know on the subject and I hope it proves useful to you.

Chapter 1

~~

Reflections on Cruising

Standing long, solitary watches at sea tends to make a sailor reflective, if not downright philosophical. Maybe a little reflection is timely right now, at the very beginning of this adventure. Let us pause to consider how to approach what we're doing. Here are some basic tenets of outfitting for world cruising, or for any long sailing voyage, that are worth cultivating into habits.

Tenet #1 - Have Fun

I always wince when someone says to me, "Oh, so you're talking about doing some really *serious* sailing." No, I'm not. I'm talking about doing some really *fun* sailing. Serious is what I hope to leave behind.

Cruising is a state of mind, an ongoing process, a lifestyle. Preparing the boat is a part of it, so start enjoying the cruising life right from the start. Outfitting for long distance voyaging is a sizeable project, but don't let it overwhelm you. Allow yourself plenty of time—it can take many months to "trick out" a boat. Just keep thinking of all the wonderful places you'll be using that gear you're accumulating. That can bring a secret smile to your lips even in the thick of a big-city rush-hour traffic jam.

Of course, you need to be conscientious in your preparations to go to sea. But remember: We don't go cruising because we have to. We go because we *want* to. Are we having fun yet?

Tenet # 2 - Plan Ahead

Planning ahead is really what this book is all about. You are endeavoring to provide for every conceivable human need, tactical predicament, maintenance routine, and mechanical breakdown that can occur while cruising, and you're preparing to cope with everything yourself without any assistance from the outside world. To do this you'll need to organize, install, and understand the necessary systems and equipment. *Ready for Sea!* is going to guide you along this worthy path. If you combine this book's suggestions with your own common sense, you will set sail with confidence, captain of a thoroughly prepared ship.

Employ a little mental visualization while you fit out your boat. When you picture any of the endless variety of situations likely to be encountered by a cruising sailor, and note what gear will serve your purposes there, you are taking a giant step toward the complete preparation of your vessel and yourself.

Tenet #3 - Be Safe

People often ask me, "Isn't it dangerous out there?" My standard answer is that, statistically, it's a lot more dangerous to drive a car cross-country than it is to cross an ocean in a well-found sailboat. Still, there are dangers inherent in sailing and we'd be foolish to ignore them. If we're wise, in outfitting as in life, we hope for the best but plan for the worst.

Chapter 7 on Safety and the many safety tips throughout this book are meant to help raise your safety consciousness. Not only must we equip our boats with safety always in mind, but we must also sail them safely as well. Educate yourself in all safety-related boating equipment and operational techniques. Let experience, your own and that of others, be your teacher and let common sense and a healthy respect for the sea be your guide.

Tenet #4 - Every complex system needs a simple, manual back up

Murphy's Law: "Anything that can go wrong, will go wrong—at the most inconvenient time."

Today, a cruising sailboat may be loaded with the marvels of modern science: electrics, electronics, roller-this and auto-that. There's much to be gained by availing ourselves of these conveniences. They can add to the fun, ease and safety of the cruise. But the more sophisticated the system, the more prone it is to failure in the abusive environment of salt air, scorching sun, and rough seas.

Inevitably, you'll be glad to have a simpler piece of gear as a back up, standing by to replace primary equipment that fails. For example, the dinghy may be propelled by an outboard motor, but you'd better also carry a pair of oars aboard for when (*when*, not if) the motor stops running. Or, when the fresh water pressure pump or electric bilge pump fail, there needs to be a hand or foot pump already in place to take over. A lead line will sound water depth when the digital depth-sounder breaks. An emergency tiller will cover temporarily for a broken steering wheel cable, and a bucket for a toilet. When the GPS packs it in, you've got to carry and know how to use a sextant for offshore navigation without electronics.

This back-up philosophy applies to every piece of essential equipment aboard. Ask yourself how you will cope when the primary gear stops working. Remember Gilling's Law: *"Murphy was an optimist."*

Tenet #5 - The preferred equipment performs more than one function

We're cramming a huge pile of gear into a very compact environment. Each piece of equipment has to earn its place aboard or be left ashore. Make a point of considering how each item might serve in an alternate capacity. By the simple installation of a Y-valve, a deck wash pump (or water pump or sump pump or engine raw water intake) might convert to an emergency auxiliary bilge pump. A bulkhead cabin heater can also heat a pot of water for tea. A spare bucket doubles as a garbage can. An electric windlass may be used to whisk a crewman aloft in a bosun's chair. We'll consider many ideas throughout this manual, but get yourself in the habit of viewing things with an eye for multi-purposes.

Tenet #6 - Integrated Systems

Integrated systems take the multiple use idea a step further. Of course, everything on a boat is inter-related, at least to the extent of having a common ultimate purpose: to create the cruising lifestyle. But some equipment particularly lends itself to interacting with other gear.

For example, I wanted a spray dodger and a bimini top for my boat, SPARROW, but I dislike the way typical pipe frameworks cage you into a cockpit, interfering with passage to the side decks. I also wanted a boom gallows to secure the boom. So the gallows became the frame on which the dodger set, as well as the forward support for a sailing awning or frameless bimini top (which also served as a rain catcher). The aft end of the awning secured to a pair of goalpost-like pipes on SPARROW's stern, which supported the radar dome on one side, and the wind generator on the other (see Figure 1). The wind generator helped feed an integrated energy system (see Chapter 13: The Integrated Energy System), which included solar panels lashed on top of the sailing awning that was fastened to the boom gallows. And so on. Try viewing your cruising sailboat as a whole, giving thought to ways that the systems and equipment can share and enhance each other's performance.

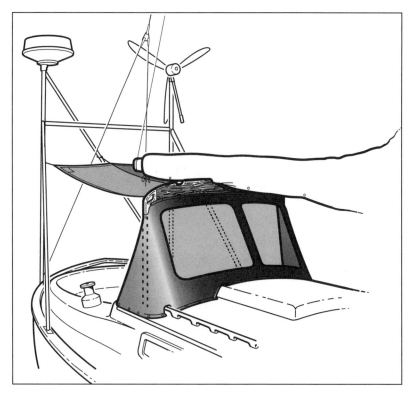

Figure 1: SPARROW's spray dodger and bimini top used the boom gallows for support, avoiding extra framework and allowing easy accesss to the side decks.

Tenet #7 - It Takes Money

It takes money to do all this. You can easily spend six figures just on the basic boat, or you can keep it small, simple and relatively inexpensive. Whether you navigate with $10,000 worth of electronics, or with a $100 plastic sextant is not so important. That you navigate accurately is. It's wiser to install less equipment of top quality than lots of lower-priced junk. It's frugal, and fun, to shop for slightly used gear at flea markets, dock sales, local trader magazines, and bulletin board ads in marinas and on the Internet (where you can also post lists of things you want to buy).

Some of what I discuss in this book are extras that can enhance liveaboard cruising but aren't absolutely necessary. If your budget is limited, strive to eliminate or compromise all but the bare essentials when outfitting (see Chapter 19: The Bare Essentials). Don't ever be discouraged from going cruising just because you don't possess every bell and whistle you read about. Joshua Slocum circumnavigated the hard way—before there was a Panama or Suez Canal—with little more than a sextant, a cheap alarm clock, a stout vessel, and the right mental attitude. If you but bring this last item aboard for your cruise, your success is virtually guaranteed.

Tenet #8 - A Word About Choosing The Boat

Strong. That's the word. All the rest is a matter of good judgment, personal inclination, and budget. Fiberglass, metal, wood, old or new, big or small, sloop, ketch, cutter, yawl or schooner? Suit yourself. But the vessel you select to carry you across oceans, in which you'll bounce off coral heads and concrete pilings, and bash through mighty seas—this vessel, her rigging, and her equipment must be tough. She must be designed, constructed (or sufficiently modified), and maintained for your purpose. Of course, the boat also needs to be an accommodating home, fun to sail, and a pleasure to behold, at least in your eyes.

Tenet #9 - Go!

I started writing this book while on a shakedown cruise from Miami to Maine, prior to setting off long-distance with Sparrow. Already several months into the cruise, I had actually done (maybe) 80% of the things this book advises you to do. I was just starting to shop for my spare parts kit, I didn't have my rain catching system together yet and there was a locker-full of equipment on board that still needed to be installed. But if I'd waited to have everything done before going cruising, I'd still be at the dock today.

Boat improvement and provisioning are a continuous process.

There are lists now of things to do, there will be lists when you cast off, and there will still be lists when you drop anchor in Bora Bora. Do all you can, get your ship as ready as possible right up to your planned departure date, then *go.* Just take the lists with you and check off more items along the way. The U.S. coasts, with their many well-stocked ports of call, provide a perfect shakedown cruise for getting started while still giving you access to equipment sources and professional assistance. In the end, underway is the best way to fine-tune your boat to suit the way you cruise.

Chapter 2

⌒⌒⌒

The Basics

In the preface I said that we're going to transform a basic *sail-away* sail-boat into an offshore cruiser. But since no two sailors (let alone two yacht brokers) agree on exactly what sail-away is, let's list the basic gear assumed to be already aboard:

Basic Equipment List

Hull, deck and coach house, rudder, keel, engine, shaft and propeller, mast, standing and running rigging, working sails, portholes, hatches, interior cabinets, wiring, lighting, plumbing, tankage, bunks, cushions, etc. In other words, a sailboat.

Plus:

- Dock lines, miscellaneous lashing lines

- Stanchions and life lines

- 4 large fenders

- Boat hook, preferably the telescoping type

- Anchor (weighing at least 1-lb. per foot of length on deck) with chain and rode

- Tell-tales on the shrouds (yarn or stocking nylon works), a wind fly, or some other non-electronic wind direction indicator

- Handrails on the coach house, grabrails belowdecks

- U.S. Coast Guard required lighting, flares, distress signals, fire extinguishers, horn, bell, life jackets

- Waterproof flashlights with batteries

- 7x50 binoculars

- Bunk bedding

- Buckets, deck brush, sponges, scouring pads

- Log book

- High hopes

Marine discount stores or their mail order or online catalogs can provide most of these items, excepting the last. Use marine equipment catalogs and periodicals, and the Internet, to learn about, compare and select boat gear. In addition to reading popular boating magazines such as *Cruising World*, *SAIL*, and *Ocean Navigator*, check out *Practical Sailor*, the "Consumer Reports" of the boating world. It offers unbiased equipment analysis, as does the Boat Owners Association newsletter of BOAT U.S.

Defender, BOAT U.S., West Marine, E&B Marine, Post Marine Supply, and JSI are among numerous discount marine catalog sales companies in the United States. To order catalogs in the U.S. you can find their 800 phone numbers through toll-free information (1-800-555-1212). Their prices for any single piece of gear may vary, so shop around for the best deal on high-ticket items.

With this basic equipment, a boat can't really *sail away*. We haven't even put the beer aboard yet. But you can go sailing, and that's as good a place as any to think about what else you'll need aboard, right? So before you go any further with your cruising preparations, or even with reading this book, take your boat out for a spin around the bay. See, we really are already having fun.

Chapter 3

~~

Up Aloft

I recall the first boat on which I ever sailed offshore, a rust-stained 34-foot steel sloop named SÜDWIND. She was owned and skippered by an unshaven Austrian guy named Horst, who signed me on in a bar in Santa Marta, Colombia, to help him sail to the Virgin Islands. Being a neophyte, I believed that all salty-looking characters with cruising-type sailboats knew what they were doing at sea, and that all cruising-type boats belonging to said characters were seaworthy. Well, guess what.

A third of the way across the Caribbean Sea, while beating hard into the winter trades, the 11-year-old rigging wire gave up the struggle with a snap. I was at the helm when it happened. I remember seeing the mast buckle at the spreaders, and topple over to leeward in what looked like slow motion. It was an awesome spectacle, but not as impressive as watching Horst, minutes later, clinging to the remaining mast stump, cutting away rigging and cursing all the while in three languages. A jury-rigged square sail and a downwind run back to Santa Marta ended the voyage for me; I flew home. Horst still faced some major repairs to his boat in a foreign port.

The whole misadventure could have been prevented, of course. The mast, the rigging, and all of the attendant fittings and gear deserve thoughtful consideration before setting sail. Once you're cruising, they continue to require periodic inspection and maintenance. So let's take a look up aloft, starting at the very top.

The Masthead

The highest point on your boat is precious space: There are lots of things that could go up there, but just these few items, if you choose to have them, really need to be there:

- Masthead tri-color running light and/or the anchor light and/or the strobe light (all are available in a single fixture)

- Masthead fly, a simple, non-electronic arrow that points into the apparent wind

- Electric wind speed instrument and/or wind direction indicator

- VHF radio antenna

- Antenna for AM/FM radio and for multi-directional television reception

- Cell phone antenna

- Pigstick halyard block for owner's pennant and yacht club burgee (not to be confused with the flag halyard beneath the starboard spreader, used for signal flags and courtesy flags)

- Lightning chaser rod (described in the Lightning Ground section of this chapter)

Single Sideband radiotelephone (SSB), ham radio and GPS antennas do not require maximum height above the water, so they can be located someplace other than at the masthead. The radar dome is most often mounted on the main mast just above spreader level. This is a reasonable compromise between its need for height and the negative effect of its weight and windage aloft.

The Mast

An aluminum mast is generally lighter and easier to maintain than a wood mast. For this reason, aluminum is the choice of most modern cruisers. Nevertheless, wooden spars have certainly earned their place offshore. Either way, you may want a separate track on the mainmast, off to one side of the mainsail track, for hoisting the storm trysail without having to remove the mainsail slides. Some aluminum mast manufacturers build in this feature.

What your mast is made of isn't as important as how you protect it from the elements. Masts of either material, if keel stepped, need good water drainage at the base to avoid corrosion there. If your boat wasn't engineered to provide for this, it's worth modifying the mast step area to drain off—not collect—water. For overall weather proofing, wood spars should ideally be UV-varnished, rather than painted, to facilitate seeing the discoloration of rotting wood before it progresses too far. Aluminum may be anodized and/or painted to protect it against oxidation.

Unstayed masts are most often made of carbon fiber and other high-tech composite materials, which are still undergoing development and the tests of time. New-wave masts, including swivel and wing masts, are logging successful voyages, but most offshore cruising sailors are pretty conservative about these things, reserving judgment for the time being. We'll take a look at slotted, Stow-Away masts a bit further on.

Standing Rigging

If my excursion aboard the ill-fated sloop SÜDWIND taught me nothing else, it indelibly impressed me with this fact: Being dismasted is no fun, especially offshore. And that contradicts Tenet #1 in this book.

Masts have got to remain standing and intact. To help keep them that way, support them with new stainless steel rigging wire or rod. For long distance offshore cruising, you might consider upsizing the wire, one size larger than the designer's specs. The useful life of rigging wire varies according to climate, lasting longer up north than in the tropics. Quality also makes a big difference in durability: Nitronic series wire is best; 316 is most commonly used and is excellent; 302 or 304 wire is inferior and has no place offshore. Solid stainless steel rod rigging is extremely strong, with the added benefit that i_t stretch like wire does, so it only needs to be tuned once w is installed.

Consult a professional rigger if you're unsure of the rigging ι .ι your boat. I would discard any 302 or 304 rigging wire immediately. I'd replace 316 wires on a boat in a warm climate every 8 or 10 years. Beyond that, you're playing Russian roulette with your mast, with the odds increasing against you. If you are outfitting a used boat for off-shore cruising, you'd be wise to replace old wire now, even if it still looks all right. It's easier to do it here and now than to put it off and have to deal with it somewhere else down the line. If you don't believe me, ask Horst. Rigging wire is not terribly expensive, so start out with a fresh set, plus one spare piece at least the length of the backstay, with the fittings necessary to use it in case of a wire breaking.

The rigging terminals used to attach the wire ends to tangs and turnbuckles are often the weak link in this vital system. The most common, the swage fitting found on the majority of modern yachts, should, in my opinion, be banned. It's responsible for many dismast-ings and many more premature re-rigging jobs, especially in warm cli-mates. During my years as a yacht broker, I've seen these rigging ends regularly fail survey on used boats when the wire was still sound. Salt and moisture get inside the fitting, corroding and cracking the wall of the swage until it ultimately suddenly lets go. Mechanical rigging ter-minals, such as the easy-to-install Sta-Lok or Norseman brand fittings, are much sounder wire end fittings (see Figures 2a and 2b). They are expensive, but they're reusable, normally out-living the rigging wire. Toggles, link fittings designed to pivot, should be installed at the lower end of at least the headstay and the backstay, and ideally on all shrouds, to prevent rigging stress from mast movement.

According to master rigger Gary Shotwell, it is better to use a turnbuckle with stainless steel threaded T-bolts and a bronze body, rather than all stainless steel. The combination is less likely to lock up from stress.

Otherwise, all of your rigging fittings should be of the same material—stainless steel. All fittings should have a breaking strength equal to or greater than that of the wire. All pins should be oversized (as most

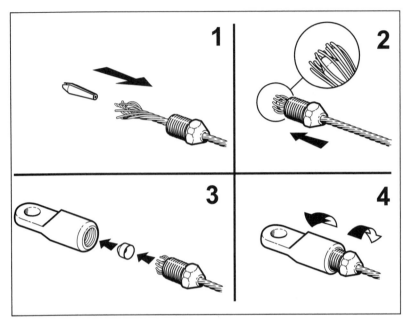

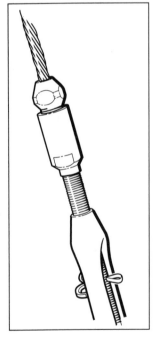

Figures 2a and 2b: Sta-Lok rigging terminals are much more reliable than common swage fittings. They require no special tools to install and are re-usable.

manufacturers make them) and match their hole size precisely. None of this will do much good if the tangs and chain plates aren't sturdy. Long, broad chain plates, through-bolted with backing plates, will best spread the enormous stresses to which they are subjected. Add baggywrinkles or other chafe gear to the shrouds where necessary to protect the boomed-out mainsail when reaching and running (more on this in the Sail section).

Make regular inspections of all rigging and fittings, looking carefully for chafe, hairline cracks, and other signs of stress. Got that, Horst?

Backstays

On some boats, a split backstay (like an inverted "Y") will open up the aft deck area and permit easier access to a windvane and transom boarding. Double-enders and broad-transom boats lend themselves to this. Double backstays (two totally separate wires) give an added safety margin of a back up if one lets go. Whether your backstay is single, split, or double, be sure to install backstay insulators (Sta-Lok brand insulators are excellent) if you plan to use long-range radios such as SSB and ham. This allows the wire to be used as a tune-able antenna. (More on this in Chapter 12 on Electronics).

Many easy-lopin' world cruisers consider quick-adjust backstay tensioning to be superfluous racing gear. In fact, tensioning the backstay a bit makes most roller-furling systems easier to operate in heavy going, and easing off the tension while in port takes unnecessary strain off the mast and rig. On a split or Y-backstay, a simple block-and-tackle adjustment system works well. Also available are mechanical and hydraulic tensioners for single backstays. Consult a professional rigger for details on these options.

Running and Intermediate Backstays

When you fly a staysail, the stay is fixed to the forward side of the foremost mast at a point between the spreaders and the masthead. The pulling force of that stay needs to be counterbalanced. Otherwise, in lumpy conditions the mast may tend to flex or pump at that point, which can eventually result in weakening and distortion of the spar. The solution is to use movable running backstays to support the mast there, or else to install permanent, intermediate backstays, which accomplish the same thing.

Which should you use, running or intermediate backstays? These are the main drawbacks of each: With moveable running backstays, you have to slacken one and tighten the other each time you tack, while with fixed intermediates, when sailing downwind, the main boom won't be able to swing out quite as far as it otherwise would because it will be stopped by the fixed wire. (Ever notice how just about every choice on a boat is a compromise?) Personally, I prefer running backstays. Since I don't tend to fly the staysail when I'm doing a lot of tacking, running backstays seem to be the lesser inconvenience.

Running backstays must be released and tightened quickly and easily while coming about. The simplest way to do this is by installing a pair of double-purchase block and tackle at the lower ends of the running back wires. The upper block on each side is shackled to the end of each stay wire. The lower block is shackled to a strong, back-plated deck padeye, located on the side deck alongside the cockpit. Each lower block should have a cam cleat that holds its line fast when it is pulled tight. As you tack, you release what was the windward running backstay line, and haul in hard and fast on what is about to become the windward backstay (it's easier than it sounds). You can lead these lines around your sheet winch to take them in, but be careful not to over-tighten them. If you really bear down on the winch, you could break the blocks.

The other system for releasing and tightening running backstays is a side-deck-mounted quick release lever. This is expensive hardware and I would recommend it only on larger boats of, say, 50 or 60 feet and up.

Inner Forestay Quick Release Lever

On many modern, cutter-rigged and staysail sloop sailboats, the inner forestay, or staysail stay, will interfere with tacking a full genoa. When coming about, the jenny has a difficult time passing through the narrow slot between the headstay and the forestay. When sailing in a situation that requires a lot of tacking, it is often handier to sail a cutter-rigged boat like a sloop, disconnecting the staysail stay at deck level and securing it off to one side.

Moving the inner forestay quickly and easily calls for a quick release lever to be installed at the lower end of the stay in lieu of a turnbuckle. When it's locked into place, the lever instantly puts the right amount of tension on the wire. To disconnect the stay from the deck so that you can move it aside, just pull the lever handle to release the wire tension. Then pull the fast pin, a kind of quick-release clevis pin, to disconnect the base of the forestay from the deck fitting. Now, you can move the forestay. By re-securing the lower end of the forestay at the base of the mast or, better still, off to the side of the mast at the boat's rail (at the base of the shrouds), you have temporarily removed this wire from the vessel's foretriangle, enabling the genoa to pass freely from side to side when you tack. The staysail stay may even be stowed with the bagged staysail still hanked on, ready for action when the forestay is re-positioned at the foredeck fitting.

It's convenient to have a padeye on the rail, to which the lever attaches, for securing the stay in its stowed-aside position. However, you'll probably find that the staysail stay is too long for the stowed position alongside the shrouds. The solution to this is to shorten the forestay wire to the correct length for clamping to its side-rail padeye, then add a short, toggled extension piece to the foredeck fitting to make up the lost length (see Figure 3).

Moving the staysail stay may be more awkward with some club-footed staysail arrangements or if the staysail is on a roller-furling system.

Running Rigging

Like standing rigging, your vessel's running rigging is a lot easier to replace at the dock than offshore. If some of your boat's sheets and halyards are looking tired or frayed, replace them now. You'll find other uses for the old lines, so coil them up and stow them in a locker. Dacron yacht braid is the modern choice for sheets; pre-stretched line is best for halyards. These new, low-stretch lines have largely replaced wire halyards on yachts. However, a wire halyard, which requires a special wire halyard winch, is excellent for hoisting a roller-furling genoa because that halyard is rarely used, the wire won't stretch, and

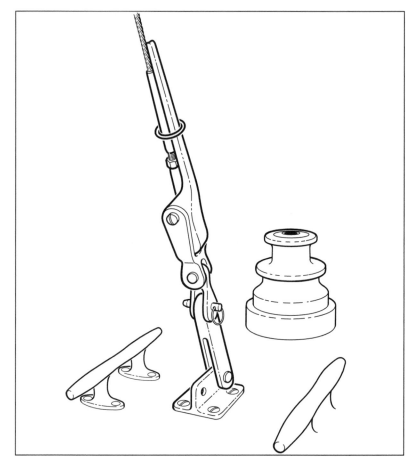

Figure 3: This removable quick release lever attaches by a fast-pin to a custom-made stainless steel extension piece on the foredeck.

there will be one less coil of line forever dangling from a cleat at the base of the mast.

Buying line by the spool saves money. Cut pieces to size as you need them and stow the rest for future use. It is often impossible to buy yacht-quality line outside of major yachting centers, especially abroad.

A halyard can break, become fouled aloft, or simply get away from you at a time when going up the mast to straighten things out is inconvenient or downright dangerous. At such times, you'll be glad you have a spare halyard in place. So, before you head out to sea, you might want to install one spare halyard for the headsail and one for the mainsail. If your halyards lead externally through fore and aft masthead sheaves, you can just install a single spare halyard that can hoist either sail. Alternatively, in lieu of spare halyards running up the mast, you can run messenger lines—1/8" nylon line will do—for reeving replacement halyards if and when needed without going aloft.

If you're installing or replacing halyard winches on your mast, you can reduce the number of winches needed to one on each side. Simply lead each halyard through a line stopper, a mechanical lever mounted on the mast above the winch that clamps down on the line and holds it fast. Each line should have its own cleat to hang on. Also, mount a winch handle holster on the mast near deck level, to keep the handle secure and handy. Self-tailing winches at the mast are preferable if your budget allows for them.

Keel-Stepped, Deck-Stepped and Tabernacle Masts

One of the favorite eternal debates among sailors is whether a mast should be stepped on deck, or stepped through the deck onto the top of the keel. Since we're focusing here on outfitting the boat you've already chosen, rather than on how to design or select the boat, and since there is no winning this argument once a skipper's mind is made up anyway, it's a moot point.

However, if your boat is designed with a deck-stepped mast, then you do have the option of adding a tabernacle system. Webster's Dictionary notwithstanding, a tabernacle is not a religious nook in the boat. A tabernacle mast step (see Figure 4) enables you to lower and raise your mast using only shipboard gear, without the aid of a boatyard crane. This allows access to bridged rivers and canals that are otherwise off limits to masted vessels. In some places, less crowded hurricane holes and boat storage facilities will become available to you, too.

Here's how a tabernacle works: Instead of stepping onto the usual collared flat deck plate, the reinforced base section of the tabernacled mast rests on a stout horizontal axle. Vertical plates welded to the deck's

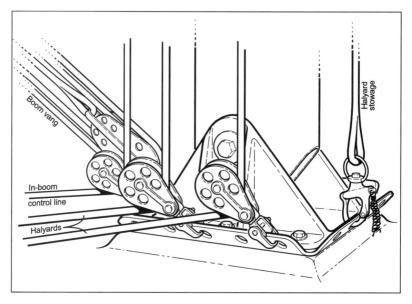

Boom vang

In-boom
control line

Halyards

Halyard
stowage

Figure 4: This tabernacle mast step is designed for the mast to pivot forward when lowered. Note the convenient block attachment holes all around the mast step collar plate.

base plate support this axle. The arrangement permits the mast to pivot on the fore and aft plane. Typically, the mast's base is cut away on the forward side, permitting it to be lowered in that direction. You can use the boom as a lever, controlled by the main sheet, for lowering and raising the mast. There should be a ring fitted in or securely lashed to each upper shroud, at the same horizontal plane as the tabernacle pin. Taut guy wires are run from the boom's aft end to these shroud pivot rings. This enables three points to pivot together when the mast is lowered, keeping the upper shrouds taut to provide side support for the mast.

A tabernacle is easy to specify as an extra when you're having a new boat built, but probably not worth tearing out an existing mast step to install unless your specific cruise plans require it.

Mast Pulpits, Lines Led Aft and Reefing Systems

Mast pulpits are guardrails on either side of the mast (see Figure 5), thru-bolted to the deck with backing plates. Ideally at about the height of your upper buttocks or lower back, they're there for you to lean against, to hold your body at the mast so your hands are free to handle lines and winches. Mast pulpits can be a real lifesaver and I recommend them if your halyards are controlled from the mast. If you decide

Figure 5: Mast pulpits hold your body at the mast, freeing your hands to handle lines and winches.

to install mast pulpits on your boat, first measure to see whether they will interfere with other deck arrangements such as carrying your dinghy on the coach house.

Alternatively, all halyards and reefing lines can be led aft to the cockpit through blocks and deck-mounted sheaves (see Figure 6). With this arrangement, you don't have to leave the safety of the cockpit to go to the mast other than to shackle on the main halyard, and there's no need for mast pulpits. It's a one-or-the-other choice.

The down side of halyards led aft is that it's harder to hoist the mainsail. There is an inevitable increase in drag due to the friction of the line making a 90° turn through a block at the mast base, and then passing through one or two sheaves to lead neatly to the cockpit. On some boats, it's the difference between being able to hoist the mainsail easily by hand (at the mast), and needing a winch— even an electric winch—to do the job from the cockpit. My own opinion is that halyards led aft are worth the extra muscle it takes to hoist the mainsail, for this reason: The mainsail reefing lines can then also be led aft, enabling you to put in and shake out reefs from the cockpit. This makes reefing easier and safer, so you'll tend to sail your boat more safely and efficiently by reefing and un-reefing earlier and more often.

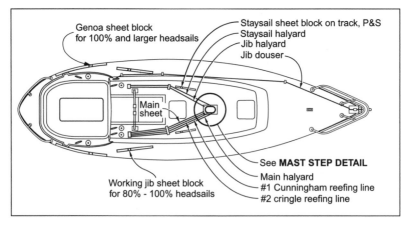

Figure 6: Leading all sail-handling lines to the cockpit makes shorthanded and singlehanded sailing easier and faster.

I'm a big fan of reefing early. When I was a younger and less prudent skipper, I once took a severe knockdown offshore because I did not reef early enough. Since then, my rule is, when you first think it might be getting near time to maybe put a reef in a sail, that's the time to do it, right then.

With so many lines coming into the forward end of the cockpit, it can quickly become a spaghetti-like jumble underway. To prevent this, be sure each line has its own line stopper mounted on the coach house just forward of the halyard winches, and provide some way to hang or stow each coiled line, either on its own cleat, or on some sort of peg, or in canvas or mesh pockets fixed along the aft side of the coach house into which each coiled line can be stuffed for containment. The point is to avoid all those lines getting tangled.

To facilitate reefing, mark your main halyard so that you can see at a glance when you have slacked it just enough to put in the first, second and third reefs. This makes your reefing procedure faster and more efficient.

Normally, there are two reef lines necessary per reef point, one to pull down the tack cringle and one to secure the clew cringle. If you opt for three reef points in your mainsail, that's six reefing lines leading under the spray dodger into your cockpit, in addition to halyards and, perhaps, a pair of staysail sheets. Even with a good line stowage system, it can become pretty crowded at the secondary winches. Here are three ideas for reducing the number of lines leading aft into the cockpit:

1. Switch to single line reefing, a system any rigger can show you that enables one reefing line to secure both the tack and clew cringles simultaneously.

2. Settle for two reef points in the mainsail instead of three by simply skipping the first (shallowest) reef.

3. Do not lead your genoa or staysail halyards aft if those sails are on roller-furling systems. What's the point? Roller-furling sails basically go up and stay up, so their halyards may as well be stowed at the mast. However, rather than installing a winch at

the mast solely devoted to tightening those halyards once a year, make the halyards long enough to pass through a snatch block at the base of the mast and reach the winches in the cockpit for tensioning. Once the roller-furling head is tensioned, secure the halyard at the mast with its own line stopper, coil the line up and hang it on its own cleat at the mast, and lash the coil to the mast so it doesn't flop around.

Mast Ladder Steps

When eyeball navigating in reef or rock infested waters, it's preferable to sight from as high above the water as possible. This enables you to read the water depths and to see submerged dangers more easily. By the way, it's best to have the sun above or behind you for this kind of navigation, and to wear polarized sunglasses to reduce water surface glare.

Steps up the mast, at least to spreader level, are the fastest way to get aloft for this, as well as for making repairs and routine inspections of the mast, rigging and equipment aloft. They create easier footing and less windage than the traditional ratlines of old, though a combination of ratlines up to the spreaders and steps continuing to the masthead also works.

Some sailors complain that external halyards become entangled in these ladder steps. Connecting all the steps' apexes, each to the next, with a taut cord or thin wire, eliminates this problem. This precaution is usually only necessary on steps above the spreaders. Another way to keep the halyards clear of the steps is to run a thin anti-fouling line from one step's apex out to the shroud and back to the next step's apex and so on, zigzagging downward.

There are two common types of steps. Stirrup-type steps provide the most secure footing, which you'll appreciate when you have to go aloft offshore with the boat pitching and rocking. Then there are the more costly fold-out steps, which collapse conveniently flat against the side of the mast and so reduce windage and don't snag halyards as readily. (See Figures 7a and b.)

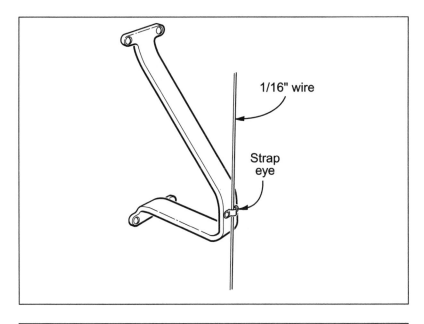

1/16" wire

Strap
eye

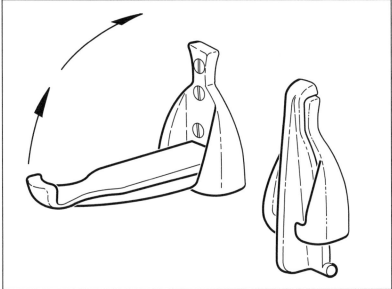

Figures 7a and b: Getting aloft is quick and easy once you have installed ladder steps up the mast. Pace-Edwards stirrup steps offer secure footing and are said to be radar reflective. Fold-out type steps collapse conveniently flat against the side of the mast to reduce windage.

I drilled, tapped, and screwed SPARROW's stirrup steps to the mast, which seems a stronger attachment than the manufacturer's alternative method of using rivets. Dipping each screw in LocTite sealant helps prevent electrolysis between the screws' stainless steel and the mast's aluminum. I installed the Pace-Edwards aluminum mast steps, advertised to be radar reflective. They are strong, broad steps with a decent tread and built-in fairleads for the anti-fouling line. My steps alternated sides at 18" intervals, with an even or level pair of steps 4 feet below the masthead for standing while working up there.

Other devices for climbing aloft, such as mast climbers (a kind of ladder hoisted by a halyard) don't seem practical for use underway, especially if the mainsail is set.

When climbing any mast, it's smart to have your rump in a bosun's chair, with your mate taking up the halyard around a winch as you ascend. It not only provides a much greater degree of safety, but allows you to use both hands to work once the chair's halyard is made fast. In addition, I wear my safety harness and tether myself to the mast while working aloft. Fear of falling is an instinct worth heeding. Don't trust a snap shackle to support you when you're aloft. Snap shackles are convenient for non-critical uses, but they've been known to let go unexpectedly. Personally, I'd trust my life to a bowline before I would to any piece of hardware.

Roller Furling/Reefing

Being conservative where offshore equipment is concerned, I was a late convert to roller furling aboard my own boat. Years ago I had problems with the early systems on several occasions during offshore deliveries. But the technology has improved to the point that these systems are truly seaworthy, as demonstrated by the many BOC Challenge participants and by countless other offshore sailors whose rigs have withstood severe tests.

So I finally treated myself to the wonderful convenience of a roller-furling/reefing headsail. It is fast and easy to increase or decrease the sail's size, which encourages quicker response to changing conditions. That translates into greater efficiency and safety underway.

The secret to getting the most out of the roller-furling/reefing headsail system is having a genoa that's made to roller-reef. A bi-radial cut headsail with a foam-padded luff fits the bill admirably, around 135-140% in size. Such a sail reefs down simply by rolling it in part way. More importantly, it can be reduced in size by 2/3 and still retain reasonably good sail shape for beating to windward, as long as the sheet block is moved forward for each stage of reefing. This turns a 140% jenny into a serviceable small working jib or yankee, eliminating cumbersome sail changes. Of course, a roller-furling headsail also reduces the number of sail bags to stow, which is a valuable space saver on a cruising boat. However, the sail must be designed to reef neatly. A genoa not intentionally cut for this will loose its shape when it's partially rolled up, bagging out in the middle and becoming useless for windward sailing.

A roller-furling genoa must have UV protection along the luff, which is constantly exposed when the sail is furled. The sail may roll more easily if the genoa halyard tension is eased just a tad, rather than being winched bowstring tight.

I personally prefer a staysail that hanks on. I confess I would probably use it more if it, too, rolled in and out, but I'd rather keep this small workhorse simple. Also I like being able to remove the inner forestay to the side when making multiple tacks with the full genoa flying. This is more difficult with a roller-furling staysail. Finally, it is onto the staysail stay that I hank and hoist the storm jib when things get really rough. A roller-furling system would make this sail change more awkward. Of course, it is easier to use a staysail that rolls in and out. The choice is yours, a trade-off either way.

Rolling up the mainsail is another matter. Decades ago, mainsail boom roller reefing was popular on sailing yachts. By means of special fore and aft end-fittings, the boom could be rolled by cranking with a winch handle at the gooseneck. The mainsail rolled around the outside of the boom and so could be reefed to any size. It sounds good, but in reality this system was slow and cumbersome and the mainsail usually had a terrible shape when reefed, becoming bagged out in the middle.

The next roller-furling/reefing mainsail system introduced, the slotted Stow-Away mast, was first popularized by Ted Hood. This system offers the same ease of handling for the mainsail as does roller furling for the genoa. The Stow-Away is an expensive spar to purchase, and it's known to whistle (howl, actually) in certain wind conditions because of the full-length slot, although this can be quieted with a hoisted cover or stopper. There are also companies manufacturing external bolt-on units that modify a normal mast for roller furling. This is an economical way to convert your rig if a roller-furling/reefing mainsail is what you want. A mainsail that rolls up around its own luff cannot have battens, and without battens a mainsail cannot carry roach. So the leech is straight and the sail less powerful. Until recently, this has been the trade-off for the convenience of a roller-furling mainsail.

Now there is an alternative mainsail roller-furling/reefing system on the market, the modern roller-furling boom. The evolved roller-furling boom is much improved over the original models of the 1950s. A fully battened mainsail can be furled and reefed inside this special spar. It doesn't require buying an entire, special mast, but the boom itself is expensive. Perhaps the best-engineered mainsail furling boom today is made by Leisure Furl International in New Zealand. This system allows for the lines to be led to operate from the cockpit, and for a big, powerful mainsail with a full roach to be handled with relative ease by a singlehanded sailor. On larger boats, an electric winch is probably a good addition to this system, especially if the lines are led to the cockpit making them harder to pull. The Leisure Furl boom necessitates a reinforced, fore and aft hole to be bored through the mast. If I were going to have a roller-furling mainsail, a boom-furling system is the way I would go.

Other modern add-ons for sailboats include the boom brake, a simple system that prevents accidental jibes and controls intentional jibes. Seems like a good idea to me if you're shopping for gismos. Also, there are rigid (hydraulic) boom vangs, which claim to obviate the traditional topping lift by supporting the boom from below. However, even if the boom is supported by a strut-type vang, a topping lift is still a wise safety precaution—a simple, manual back up to a modern gadget. Visit a rigging shop, chandlery or boat show to look over these devices. Then decide for yourself what makes sense for you. Just remember that for every advocate who swears by the gadget, there are a hundred who cruise successfully without it.

Whisker Poles and Twin Headsails

A whisker pole holds out the jib or genoa clew when broad reaching or running on a bouncy sea or in light air. This prevents the sail from constantly collapsing and filling as the ship rolls. There are various ways to mount and deploy whisker poles. A stroll through any large marina, or a visit to your local rigger, will provide you with examples of how these systems are set up. Basically, a track is securely mounted on the forward side of the foremost mast. On this track rides a car with a hefty ring to which one end of the whisker pole is attached. The sliding car enables you to adjust the height of the pole's inboard end so it's level with the sail's clew, to which the outboard end of the pole is attached when in use. Fore and aft guy lines, running from the outboard end of the pole to deck fittings, hold the pole down.

I've learned the hard way that spring-loaded end fittings of seldom used poles will seize up rock solid from salt build-up when stowed at deck level (soaking them in vinegar overnight may dissolve the salt and free up the fitting). It's best to stow poles a few feet above the coach house, either on the mast or in the shrouds. This reduces the salt build-up from deck-level spray. Rinse the end fittings well with fresh water whenever you can and lubricate the moving parts periodically with a waterproof lubricant.

A pair of whisker poles can serve to hold out twin jibs, used for downwind sailing. That is a practical, well-balanced sail configuration for tradewind cruising. In order to fly twin jibs or genoas, you need a second jib halyard in place, and an additional whisker pole car on the mast track. Also required is a second headstay on which to hank the second headsail, or a second slot available in the roller-furling system's headstay foil. Carrying a spare genoa on long voyages is a good idea anyway if you can afford the cost and stowage space. If you carry a spare, you might as well set the boat up for flying twin headsails.

Lazy Jacks

I don't know why lazy jacks aren't more popular aboard sailboats these days. They're as functional as they are traditional. When the mainsail is dropped, lazy jacks catch it in a net of line, keeping it from flailing and falling on deck to block the helmsman's view just when he most needs to see where he's going. With the mainsail thus contained, furling can wait until anchoring or docking maneuvers are completed.

Ideally, the main lazy jacklines run from the boom's aft end, up to small blocks on the underside of the spreaders about 1/3 of the way out from the mast, rather than on the sides of the mast itself, and then down to small cleats lashed onto the forward lower shrouds. You might want to fasten cable clamps to the shrouds, just beneath the spreader tips, to ensure the spreaders won't be pulled downward if someone yanks on the lazy jackline. Running the lines to the spreaders widens the net (compared to lines running to the mast), and it keeps the lines away from the mast so they don't slap in a breeze. The cleated ends permit adjustment of the lazy jacks. Vertical or inverted-Y lines run from the main lines, underneath the boom, to form the net (see Figure 8). By untying the main lines from the boom, the whole system can slide forward to the mast, out of the way, for rigging a full awning over the boom while at anchor. On the down side, when hoisting the mainsail, lazy jacks may snag the batten ends if the boat isn't headed directly into the wind.

If you want to spend the extra money, there are one or two commercially available sail-catchment systems around, such as the Doyle Stack-Pack. This flakes the mainsail neatly as it drops, and reportedly works well enough. However, you'll need a specially cut awning to fit over the boom with this sail catchment system in place. Also, the boat must be headed directly into the wind to lower the mainsail, which may be proper practice but is not always practical.

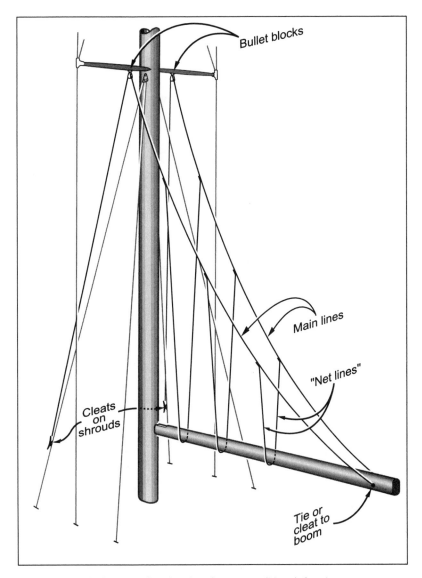

Figure 8: Lazy jacks are as functional as they are traditional, forming a net to catch the mainsail when it is lowered.

Flags

Flying flags is fun—and that fits into our philosophy of cruising. Sure, you can lash Q-flags and courtesy flags to a shroud, I suppose. But go ahead and rig a simple flag halyard to the starboard spreader, and maybe invest in a set of international signal flags. Learn a little flag etiquette: *Chapman's Piloting, Seamanship, and Small Boat Handling* has a section on it. If you don't have a yacht club burgee, design an owner's private pennant of your own to fly at the masthead from a "pigstick" hoisted aloft on its own halyard. Fly a Sunday Jack forward once a week, and on holidays. For special holidays, employ the signal flags to spell out some appropriate word like "F-R-E-E-D-O-M" on July 4th, or "S-A-I-L-N-A-K-E-D" at Antigua Race Week—just for fun. Of course, always fly your national ensign aft, and carry spares because it'll weather and wear out while cruising in foreign waters where it is often a requirement to exhibit, but impossible to buy.

Unofficially, a flag halyard to the port spreader can be used to fly personal and miscellaneous flags, such as your signal flags, a cruising club burgee, an ecology flag, a cocktail hour flag, or whatever you're into. Also, when foreign guests are sailing aboard, you may fly their country's ensign below the port spreader to honor or announce their presence, but hoist it a bit lower than the courtesy flag flying to starboard. I have collected quite an array of colorful flags for this unofficial port flag halyard—just the thing for dressing ship on special occasions.

A courtesy flag is the merchant ensign (which is often, but not always, the same as the national ensign) of the host country you are visiting with your boat. Flown just below the starboard main spreader, it is often required and always good form while in foreign waters. The world cruiser will need courtesy flags for each country he visits. This can be a formidable collection; difficult to obtain prior to arrival, and wasteful if one brief visit is the flag's only use.

Consider instead carrying a bag-full of cloths of various colors. Scraps of spinnaker nylon are excellent flag-making materials (I got all the scraps I wanted from a sail loft for a six-pack of beer). These can be quickly sewn, or even contact-glued together, to approximate the host country's ensign and will pass admirably once hoisted aloft. Intricate flag designs can be drawn with colorfast ink onto clear Rip-Stop sail repair tape, cut to shape and stuck onto the flag. A grommet set will enable you to finish off your flags professionally. Later, the flag may be disassembled and the cloth re-cycled. Carry a United Nations chart of national and merchant ensigns to provide patterns for copying, so you can make the flags en route, before you arrive in a new country.

Deck Lights

Inevitably, you will find yourself fumbling about on the foredeck on a dark, rough night. You'll need to see what you're doing and you won't want to hold a flashlight in your hand, or mouth, or armpit. A deck light mounted on the forward mast around spreader level, sometimes combined in a single unit with the steaming light (also called the bow light), is the solution. Spreader lights will work as well if you can keep them aimed where you want them and not in the helmsman's eyes. The deck light can also be used to make your little vessel more visible to big vessels passing too close at night. You might install a rheostat (a dimmer switch) to control deck or spreader light brightness to suit different occasions.

All electrical wires from the mast should lead through waterproof connectors or a watertight junction box at the base of the mast, so that they can be disconnected, rather than cut, when the mast is unstepped.

While we're on the subject of lights: carry a powerful 12-volt, handheld spotlight aboard and install a socket near the foredeck as well as in the cockpit. The cockpit plug socket can serve double, even triple duty: Sometimes I like to read in the cockpit during night watches at sea (a 360-degree glance around every few minutes gives plenty of warning of approaching ships). Rather than wasting flashlight batteries for this, I use a moveable 12-volt chart table light with a polarized dimmer lens. I installed the same plug on it as is on the big 12-volt spotlight, so I simply plug the reading light into the spotlight socket in the cockpit. In port, a 12-volt lamp using the same socket can hang from the boom to provide a cockpit light for evening meals and socializing.

Tri-Color Masthead Light

The most dangerous thing on the ocean for the cruising sailor isn't storms, reefs, pirates, or sea monsters. It's the danger of collision with a large ship. However, those giants are much less likely to run you down if the mariner on watch sees you. So, help him by showing your running lights up high when under sail with a tri-color light at the masthead. This puts the lights much nearer to his eye level and keeps them from disappearing so readily behind waves.

A single-bulb tri-color light draws less electrical power than the two- or three-bulb deck-level alternative. As an added bonus, if positioned properly, it'll illuminate the masthead fly so the helmsman can read the relative wind direction at night.

Of course, you'll still use deck level running lights when you're motoring, instead of the tri-color, because the rules require the white steaming (bow) light to be higher than the colored running lights. Remember, too, that running lights at your masthead are not so visible to small, nearby craft in a harbor as are your deck level lights. The tri-color is primarily for offshore use while sailing, but very effective for that.

An alternative arrangement of running lights when under power offshore is accomplished by turning on the deck level port and starboard lights, and the all-around masthead anchor light. This essentially meets the requirements for lighting with a couple of advantages: The anchor light is higher—and therefore more visible to ships—than the normal bow and stern lights, both of which it will replace in this case. This will also get rid of the glare of the deck-level stern light, which often restricts night vision astern. This alternate lighting calls for the installation of a separate on/off switch for the deck-level stern light, which otherwise normally comes on with the port and starboard running lights.

Strobe Lights

Unfortunately, strobe lights have been assigned the status of emergency or distress lights on vessels (except on hovercraft) by international authorities. For the cruising sailboat, there is no better way to attract attention and announce its presence on a dark sea. However, cruisers being an independent lot, some let their masthead strobe light flash throughout the night when passage-making offshore, especially in waters frequented by ships. Perhaps they figure it's a case of placing the safety of their boat and crew above the rules and regulations. I haven't yet heard of an instance where another vessel has responded to a strobe light as a distress signal when it's used in this way, though I suppose it could happen. If you use a strobe light this way, use it *in addition to* the running lights.

Radar Reflector

Another way to help ships see your vessel is by carrying a radar reflector aloft in the rigging. Some reflectors are made to mount permanently on the mast, others to be hoisted on a halyard. On SPARROW I used an inexpensive Davis aluminum radar reflector hoisted to spreader level by the port flag halyard, with a lashing sideways to the shroud to prevent it from spinning (watch out for chafing of the flag halyard against the reflector's edge). A radar reflector makes your boat more visible to a ship's radar. You'd be wise to use one.

Lightning Ground

Twice in 10 years I was anchored next to boats that were struck by lightning. One of them belonged to a guy who was bitten by a shark that same week. Maybe Somebody was trying to tell him something, though I'm not sure what.

There are various theories about how and why lightning strikes a sailboat and what happens when it does. Personally, I think it's something between you and your Maker, but let's at least do what we can not to aggravate the situation.

Many yacht designers and builders ground the mast and rigging. That is, they provide a direct conductive metal connection to the sea to neutralize the air around the boat by draining off its charge. This seems to work pretty well, but it doesn't guarantee protection. The builder may run heavy copper cables inside the hull from the chainplate backing plates down to the bilge. Here the cables fasten to a bolt passing through the hull to an underwater dynaplate. This plate has a porous, convoluted surface that presents a lot of surface area in a small space to facilitate dissipation of current into the sea.

The old fashioned way to accomplish this grounding is to simply clamp one end of a copper cable, such as an automobile jumper cable with the ends stripped to bare wire, to the base of an upper shroud. Then trail the other stripped end in the water when lightning is around.

It's prudent to disconnect all power and antenna wires from electronics when lightning is occurring, to reduce damage in the event of a strike. There are in-line interrupter devices on the market that supposedly will prevent a lightning electrical surge from damaging electronic equipment, but they're not always effective according to at least one first-hand report from a cruising acquaintance of mine who had all his electronics blown away in spite of the interrupters he had installed.

There is, or used to be, a lightning strike preventer on the market called the Lightning Chaser De-Ionization Rod. It is said to form *a cone of protection* over your vessel, making the area less inviting to a lightning bolt. Perhaps it enhances the grounding system. Who knows? I mounted one on SPARROW, but I still whispered a little prayer in lightning storms.

Chapter 4

Sails, Canvas and Drogues

Sails

The wings of man! Years ago I owned a classic, 50-year old, William Hand designed gaff rigger, the ketch AUTANT. She was engine-less; sail was her only means of propulsion. What a beauty she was! People would scramble for their cameras when she swept into a harbor under a full press of canvas.

Home base in those days was the Dinner Key free anchorage in Coconut Grove. There was a whole community of us longhaired live-aboards of modest means trying to get our old wooden ships together and provisioned enough to wander off to the islands. Often when parting company, instead of saying to each other "Goodbye", or "See you later", we would say "Reef early" as our standard farewell. I can think of no better advice regarding the handling of sails on a cruising sailboat.

Factors that apply most critically to your ship's sails are initial quality, protection against the damaging effects of sunlight, and protection against chafe. Quality begins at the design board, then with the sail-cloth, and finally lies in the hands of your sailmaker. Seek out a highly regarded sailmaker in your area. Then sit down with him over a cup of coffee and discuss what you want, and what he suggests you need. If your boat came with serviceable sails, have them thoroughly checked over and reconditioned by a professional before setting off on a long voyage.

The UV rays of the sun cause severe deterioration of sailcloth and stitching. A cruising boat's sails should be constructed from sailcloth and sail thread that has been chemically treated to filter out UV light rays. Because the leech and foot of roller-furling headsails are always exposed, they need to have a sacrificial layer of UV-resistant cloth, such as Sunbrella awning fabric, sewn over with treated thread. It's up to you to always keep all other sails completely covered or bagged when not in use. Be careful, especially in the tropics, that no clew or head is poking out of the covering. Otherwise, guess which part of the sail will fail first.

To protect your sails against chafe, put baggywrinkles or similar chafe protection on the shrouds where the mainsail touches during broad reaches and runs. My friend and illustrator, Bruce Bingham, describes how to install a neat, modern substitute for bulky, traditional baggywrinkles in *The Sailor's Sketchbook*. It involves lashing strips of 1" closed cell foam rubber, wrapped corkscrew fashion around the shrouds in key locations (see Figure 9). Have sacrificial chafe patches sewn over the forward foot area of your genoa if it rubs against the bow pulpit. Do the same for any other places that chafe. Sail repair tape can sometimes serve as a cheap, easy, but only temporary chafe patch when you discover new chafe spots. You'll be amazed at how quickly chaffing fabric suffers on long passages.

Sail Inventory List

- 135-140% genoa, bi-radial cut, with foam-padded luff for roller reefing. This versatile headsail, set on a sturdy roller-furling system, replaces all the genoas, yankees, and working jibs that sailors used to lug along on a cruise. Thanks to the foam-padded luff, the headsail can be roller-reefed down to 1/3 its full size to suit the wind force, yet still maintain a good shape as long as the sheet block is moved forward as the sail's size is decreased.

- Second genoa identical to the first (if budget and space permit). This sail is stowed in a locker. It is a spare, a back-up for the primary headsail, without which the boat could not

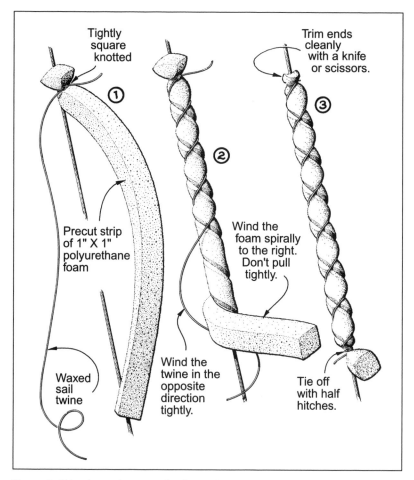

Figure 9: This trim replacement for the traditional "mop head" baggywrinkle prevents sail chafe. It is a strip of closed cell foam wrapped around a shroud, lashed in place with stout sail twine.

sail well to windward. It may also be flown along with the primary headsail for double-headsail downwind cruising (see Whisker Poles in Chapter 3).

- Cruising (pole-less) spinnaker. This asymmetrical spinnaker is not necessary for cruising, but it adds versatility and pizazz to light air sailing. A sleeve furler or spinnaker sock, such as the

ChuteScoop, makes this sail much easier to use than it otherwise would be, especially for a shorthanded crew.

- Staysail (in my case, hanked on and with reef points). This is the offshore workhorse of the modern cutter or staysail sloop. It may be flown virtually all the time during an offshore passage while the genoa and mainsail are reefed and unreefed to suit the wind strength. Reefed down, the staysail makes a serviceable storm jib.

- Storm jib, with sheets already attached, set on the staysail stay. Every offshore cruising sailboat ought to have one for heavy weather work, although if the cruise is entirely in the gentler latitudes a staysail that can be reefed down may serve the same purpose. A storm jib with luff straps instead of hanks can be set over a furled roller-furling staysail.

- Storm trysail, with sheets already attached, a dedicated mast track, and also grommets for lashing to the mast if the cars fail. Like the storm jib, it's necessary to have aboard, though seldom used in moderate latitudes.

- Mainsail with at least two sets of reef points. I had read that full-length battens in a mainsail improve the sail's performance, and so I ordered a fully battened main for SPARROW. My opinion after 30,000 fully battened miles? If full-length battens are already there, fine. If not, don't blow your budget to convert your sail. On an offshore cruising sailboat, the pros and cons pretty much balance out. While full-length battens do improve the efficiency of the mainsail a bit in light winds, they can be a minor hindrance when raising and lowering the sail. Also, the batten pockets tend to chafe.

On split-rigged vessels—ketches and yawls—the mizzen sail should have at least one set of reef points, especially if you use it for heaving-to. These boats will also benefit by adding a mizzen staysail to the inventory. This easy-to-handle sail can give you an extra knot in light airs.

Tanbark sails aren't seen much these days, except on the occasional, classic-style yacht. With their dark red mahogany coloring, they sure do stand out in a crowd. In the days of yore, tanning was done to preserve the life of the canvas fabric by dressing it with cutch, which produced the color. With today's synthetic sailcloths, the only useful function of tanbark sails is to reduce the glare of sunlight and to look classic.

Tell-tales

Tell-tales are typically 6" to 10" lengths of colored yarn, taped to sails in pairs, on either side of the sail. When pairs of tell-tales are streaming aft together in parallel, they indicate that the wind is flowing evenly along both sides of the sail, so you can see that the sail is set most efficiently. Reading tell-tales is the only way I know to fine trim a sail for maximum sailing efficiency.

I suggest you put tell-tales on all sails. Install three pair evenly spaced up the genoa, parallel to and a foot or so back from the luff. Also, attach two pair six to ten feet back from the luff of the jenny for when the sail is reefed. Another two pairs belong on the staysail. Place them a foot or so back from the luff. On the mainsail, place two pairs near the luff, and two more near the leech. Some 8" lengths of red and green knitting yarn and some sticky patches cut from Rip-Stop sail repair tape are all you need to make and mount your own tell-tales.

You can also tie tell-tales to the main shrouds as a simple wind direction indicator.

Canvas Accessories

Canvas accessories are not canvas at all these days, but acrylics and other synthetics. Choose your fabric color thoughtfully because you will live with it all around you for a long time. Use only UV-treated cloth. Seek out the best canvas shop in your area by asking local opinions. Then sit down with the owner and discuss what you're setting out to do, and what you need from him. Here is the canvas package I used aboard SPARROW. It served me well for six years and 30,000 miles:

Canvas Inventory List

- A spray dodger with clear plastic windows. The center window section zipped open and rolled up in mild weather. There were clear plastic pockets in the side flaps for sunglasses, etc., with a small water drain grommet at the bottom of each pocket. SPARROW's dodger was framed by the boom gallows. It looked unusual—not as sleek as some spray dodger designs—but it worked well.

- Removable sunscreen covers for the dodger's plastic windows. Using these snap-on nylon screen panels in port increased both cockpit privacy and the life span of the plastic, while dampening glare.

- A bimini top or sailing awning. Necessary to protect the crew from tropical sun, SPARROW's frameless cockpit awning also had a hose fitting sewn in for channeling collected rain water, through a hose, directly to a water tank deck fill. This awning also had lashing lines sewn on top to secure a pair of flexible solar panels.

- A cockpit side panel. I used a single fabric panel to protect just the windward side of the cockpit, making it a more habitable place to sit when sailing in foul weather. This was in lieu of a complete cockpit enclosure. The panel was made to be reversible and so worked on either the port or starboard side, whichever was to windward. My side panel attached to the dodger, the bimini, the cockpit coaming and the aft pole mounts and formed a wall against the elements when beating in rough, wet conditions. This permitted me to sit in the cockpit without being constantly harassed by the wind and soaked by spray and rain. A clear plastic window let me peek out for ships to windward without getting a face-full of seawater for my trouble.

- Full cockpit enclosure. Since sailors spend so much time in the cockpit, it pays to make it a pleasant place to be in all weather conditions. I did not have a full cockpit enclosure on my last boat, but I expect I will on my next one, rather than the single cockpit side panel. The enclosure consists essentially of three removable Sunbrella panels with large, clear vinyl windows. The panels are usually attached to the bimini, the spray dodger and each other by zippers, and at their bottom edge by snap fittings along the cockpit coaming. The aft panel can double as a late afternoon cockpit sunshade when in port if you fit window covers over the clear vinyl.

- A reinforced deck awning that sets above the boom, just overlapping the bimini. The shade this provides keeps the boat's interior much cooler in tropical harbors. The forward end lashes to the mast and shrouds. A stiff batten slides into a long pocket sewn across the aft end to make it rigid, and then is hoisted (up and aft) by a line through a block lashed onto the backstay. Hose fittings are sewn into the belly of the awning, port and starboard, for rainwater collection. Flexible solar panels can be lashed on.

- A small foredeck awning. This permits the forward hatch to remain open even in the rain, providing welcomed ventilation while at anchor in warm climates.

- Splash screens, also called weather cloths. These panels lash to the lifelines beside the cockpit and not only ward off sea spray, but also block a great deal of the sunlight glare reflected from the water's surface. In addition, they increase privacy in the cockpit. You can sew pockets onto the inside to hold small items. The outside of the cloths can bear the boat's name or racing number, a requirement in some ocean races.

- Lee cloths for the port and starboard settees. They will keep the crew in a windward bunk while the boat is heeled.

- Sail bags for the staysail and storm trysail. On SPARROW, these bags were designed so that the staysail could remain hanked on when bagged on deck, and the bagged storm trysail could stow ready in its track, at the base of the mast, with sheets attached. Install a grommeted water drainage hole in the bottom of these sail bags to keep them from filling up with water in heavy weather.

- Multi-directional Windscoops. They will bring fresh air into overhead hatches while the vessel is in port.

- Sunbrella covers. For the mainsail, the liferaft canister, the barbecue, the outboard motor, the on-deck water and fuel jugs, the dinghy (if carried upright), the water heater and cabin heater Charlie Nobles, the anchor windlass, the winches, etc. Winch covers can reduce maintenance by prolonging the life of the grease inside the winches. If you use light-colored covers, they will keep the sun off and the heat down, thus limiting or avoiding the melting of grease, which otherwise runs off when it liquefies.

Drogues, Sea Anchors and Warps

If you're forced to run before heavy weather, it may become necessary to slow the boat's progress. You may want to limit the distance traveled in that direction, or prevent excessive surfing for better steering control and to reduce the tendency of the boat to broach or pitchpole. This is usually accomplished by towing a drogue astern to create sufficient drag in the water. Drogues are improvised or manufactured contraptions of various design; anything from a sail and yardarm dragged on a long line, to a professionally made canvas scoop or parachute with a swivel tow fitting and trip line.

When you are heaving-to and wish to keep the boat's bow to the wind and sea, it is recommended that you use a sea anchor, a drogue deployed from the bow. However, there's some debate about whether this is safe, or even effective, on a deep-keel sailboat. I've never tried it myself.

One excellent production drogue for yachts is the Galerider. It's a strong cone of nylon webbing on a proper swivel, a no-nonsense piece of storm equipment that I carried, but never did use, aboard SPARROW. It is designed for deployment astern; the manufacturer warns against using it as a bow sea anchor.

Alternatively, you could tow 200 feet or more of heavy line, such as a spare anchor line, to create drag underway. Streaming the line aft is called *towing warps*. This technique is more effective when the line is towed in a bight, a long loop with each end of the line made fast to each (port and starboard) quarter cleat, or to each sheet winch, to help hold the stern to the sea and slow down the boat. You may find that you have even better steering control if the line is attached to each midship cleat instead. A weight, such as an anchor, may be attached at the trailing end of the loop to keep the line underwater and increase drag, although a huge, breaking sea could conceivably fling this weight into the boat. Tying knots at intervals along the line will further increase its drag effect, but may be hard to take out later.

Car Tires

I've heard of car tires being effectively used as a drogue or sea anchor. Certainly, if you've room, you might carry a couple of old tires aboard as heavy-duty fenders. They're cheap, rugged protection against concrete bulkheads, steel girders, old barges—the kind of things against which you may find yourself docking from time to time once you forsake the gilded marina route. Tires are particularly useful when traversing canals, such as in Europe. If covered with canvas, tires won't blacken your topsides. Large, heavy-duty plastic trash bags may serve as temporary covers if the tires are being used only briefly, such as during a Panama Canal transit.

Car tires also make excellent, strong shock absorbers for mooring and dock lines when a surge is present. Secure the tire midway between two lines, one line running from the boat to the tire, and the other from the tire to the mooring ring or dock cleat.

Chapter 5

The Deck

The deck of a sailboat ought to do much more than just keep water out of the cabins—though some of them don't even do that very well. The deck and cockpit provide at least 50% of the living and working environment aboard a cruising sailboat, so they should be arranged and equipped in a functional, convenient, and comfortable manner. The deck also supports a lot of equipment. Let's consider some common and uncommon features that can enhance the deck, both offshore and in port.

Stern Arches and Mounts

A custom, stern-mounted radar and antenna arch, if tastefully designed, can be both aesthetically pleasing and functional aboard a cruising yacht. Made of stainless steel or heavy-gauge aluminum and thru-bolt mounted, it arcs across the afterdeck just above head level (see Figure 10). On it are mounted all the antennas that don't go aloft. It may also support forward-facing deck spotlights, fishing rod holders, solar panels, radar and a wind generator. You can even incorporate dinghy davits into the design. Only the strongest antenna arches can support davits or a full-size wind generator.

It's more common to see the wind generator mounted on a single pole on the afterdeck. Aboard SPARROW, I made an unusual bi-pole

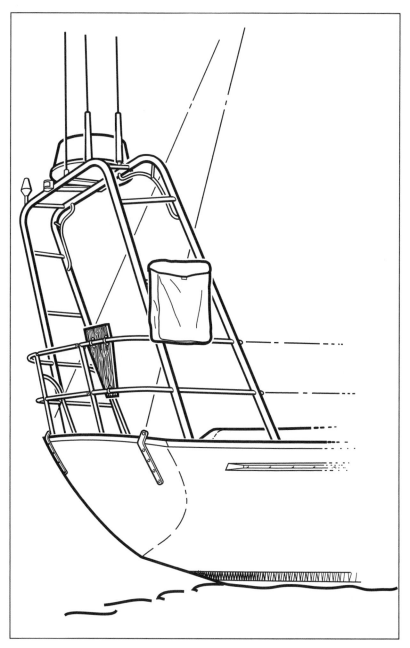

Figure 10: A well designed stainless steel antenna arch can be as aesthetically pleasing as it is functional.

mount for supporting the wind generator, the radar and antennas. It started with my desire to have a swivel-mounted wind generator permanently erected on a pole on the quarterdeck. Then I decided to lower the weight and windage of the radar scanner by also mounting it on a pole aft rather than on the mast aloft. So I had port and starboard quarterdeck poles to erect. It became apparent that they'd be much stronger if I connected them with a crossbar, like a football field goal post. Finally, ultimate strengthening by triangulation called for the addition of a diagonal crossbar and forward struts.

The resulting bi-pole stern mount (see Figures 11a and 11b) was extremely stout, as it had to be to support the heavy, whirling Windbugger in rough sea conditions. The painted, schedule-40 aluminum poles were stepped through the deck onto massive wood blocks shaped and fiberglassed to the side of the hull in the lazarette. The entire structure was assembled with split-pipe couplings, fashioned by a competent welder and which bolted together. So I could disassemble and remove it if, for example, I wished to reduce the boat's height for traversing low-bridged canals. In addition to supporting the radar and wind generator, the assembly's crossbar could carry antennas for navigational electronics such as GPS.

Boom Gallows/Bimini

The boom gallows seems to be out of vogue on modern yachts. Its primary function is to secure the boom when the mainsail is furled. Without it, no matter how tightly you snug down the main sheet, the boom will still wobble when the boat rocks. A gallows can also save the skull of the helmsman if the topping lift ever lets go. I once saw this accident occur on a boat without a boom gallows, with disastrous results.

SPARROW's custom boom gallows provided a strong handhold when leaving the cockpit to go forward. It stood on heavy gauge bronze pipes that I had bent to shape by a welding shop (stainless steel pipes will work just as well). The teak cross-timber was cut and shaped by a local boat builder, and the bronze end fittings and deck mounts were ordered from an ABI catalog.

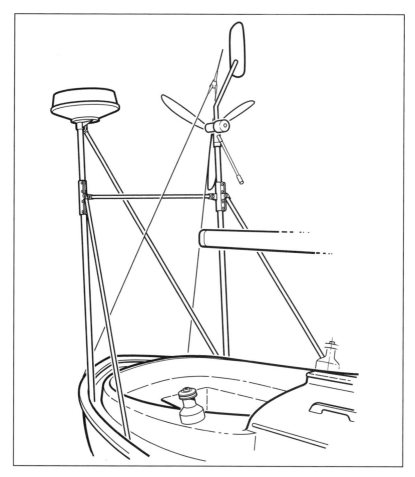

Figure 11a: SPARROW's sturdy bi-pole stern mount was custom made to support the radar and the heavy wind generator. It was also a good place to mount navigational antennas, tie off the frameless bimini top, and do my chin-ups!

My boom gallows supported the spray dodger and the front end of the bimini top. The money I saved by eliminating the normal, costly framework for this canvas entirely paid for the custom boom gallows.

Depending on the rig, there are several ways to support the aft end of a frameless bimini top, which is sometimes called a cockpit sailing

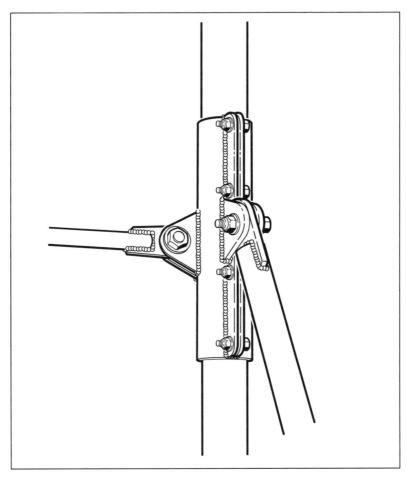

Figure 11b: I had the bi-pole stern mount's split pipe couplers made to unbolt so I could easily disassemble and take down the entire mount. This feature would be a great convenience for traveling through the canals of Europe.

awning: (1) a batten lashed to the backstay(s), with end stabilizer lines to the lifelines or to deck fittings; (2) bi-poles, either moderate and removable or stout and fixed to support additional equipment as described above; or (3) a second boom gallows aft. You can, of course, run a frameless bimini top from a normal spray dodger, as well, led back to a boom gallows on the afterdeck.

Winches and Cleats

The only acceptable excuse for not having oversized, two- or three-speed self-tailing primary jib sheet winches on any modern sailboat is the expense, which is considerable. If your boat is equipped with plain winches and you can afford to replace them with self-tailers, then treat yourself to a piece of equipment that will enhance all your future sailing days. If your budget doesn't allow for self-tailing winches, at least get Winchers, an inexpensive rubber rim add-on, available in many chandleries, that converts an ordinary winch into a semi self-tailer. These rings do free you from actually tailing the line, but you must manually guide the tail clear of the standing part after every few cranks of the winch handle. Otherwise, the sheet line wraps under itself, causing an awkward line jam.

Cleats on a cruising boat have to be strong, large, well bedded and thru-bolted to backing plates. Care must be taken that all lines will run chafe-free to and from each cleat. Many boats are built without midship deck cleats, and these need to be added. Four foredeck cleats aren't too many—one for each anchor, plus port and starboard dock line cleats.

Anchor Windlass

A cruising sailboat's ground tackle has to be substantial, which means heavy. It will sometimes be used in deep-water anchorages where getting it back aboard may require mechanical assistance. There are ways to use a sheet winch for this, but in my experience a good windlass is necessary equipment for the voyaging sailor.

You must choose between a vertical and a horizontal windlass. I prefer the vertical electric windlass because its components are entirely stainless steel above deck, and its electric motor is mounted below the deck. Some horizontal electric windlass motors are encased in a box made of coated aluminum, which will eventually corrode and may leak. Also in favor of vertical windlasses is their lower profile; they take up less space on the foredeck. A manual vertical windlass would not be so handy as it must be cranked from a kneeling position. It works faster than jacking a horizontal windlass, but unless the vertical windlass has two-speed gearing, it takes a strong person to use it manually.

I installed my electric windlass with some ribbing from friends about getting old and lazy, but am I ever glad I did go electric. It takes all the back straining and grunting out of weighing anchor. Because it's quick and easy, I'm inclined to weigh and re-set an anchor more readily, an added safety factor.

It is necessary to match the size chain you buy to the windlass chain gypsy (or else select the gypsy to fit your existing chain). If the chain and gypsy aren't compatible the windlass won't be able to hold your chain at all. When planning anchor chain storage, remember that a vertical windlass will generally feed chain to port; a horizontal windlass to the starboard side of a divided chain locker (see Figures 12a and 12b).

An electric windlass does, of course, consume electrical power in big gulps. It requires special wiring and, ideally, a separate, designated battery. A starter battery works fine, deep cycle being unnecessary for this application. In Chapter 13, which covers the integrated energy system, we'll examine the placement and wiring of the electric windlass' battery.

In addition to weighing anchors, a bow windlass can be used in conjunction with a halyard to hoist a crewmember aloft, or a dinghy aboard. It can pull the bow off a leeward dock with a line to a piling, and facilitate kedging off when you've run aground. A windlass is a strong piece of machinery that earns its place aboard any voyaging sailboat.

Ground Tackle and Mooring Lines

On many modern yachts, the bow anchors stow in bow rollers on the stem head, a very practical feature. It eases the struggle and back strain of anchor handling, and solves the anchor stowage problem neatly. You'll want double rollers, one for each of your two bow anchors. The installation should offer a way to pin, lock, lash or otherwise secure the anchors in place against heavy weather underway. Also, a deck-

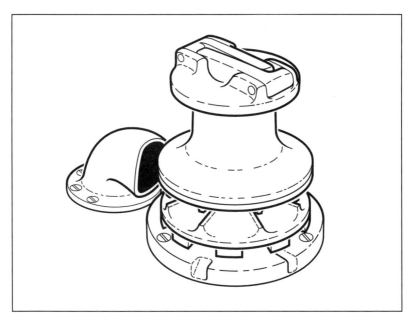

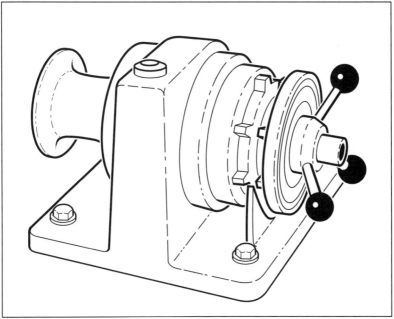

Figures 12a and 12b: A vertical windlass feeds chain to the port side of the chain locker; a horizontal windlass to the starboard side.

mounted chain lock device is a good idea for securing the chain when the boat is anchored. Avoid using the windlass for this because excessive strain, such as sudden snubbing of the anchor chain in a surge, could damage the windlass or its mounts.

The deck pipes, through which anchor chain and rode pass into the chain locker, are rarely watertight, but they should be, especially if the chain locker drains into the bilges. I've used waterproof, reusable Plasticine modeling clay (plumber's putty works, too) to seal anchor deck pipe caps when underway.

If you feel you want to line your chain lockers to protect the inside of the hull, you might consider using UHMW (ultra high molecular weight) plastic. Some commercial fishermen use it for a number of applications where impact or abrasion is a problem. It is supposed to get denser the more you beat on it and is said to stand up very well to extreme abuse. UHMW plastic comes in all kinds of shapes and colors and may be available from a commercial plastics vendor.

Good ground tackle is a boat's best insurance policy. It's smart to use heavier gear than that which is recommended by boat and anchor manufacturers. For a moderate to heavy displacement 40-foot boat, this would be my optimum ground tackle selection:

- On the bow, one 45 or 60 lb. CQR (or a 44 or 66 lb. Bruce) anchor on an all-chain rode (at least 200 feet of 3/8" Superlink or High Test galvanized chain) with an additional 200 feet of 5/8" 3-strand nylon rode in reserve and already made up with a thimbled eyesplice and shackle, for really deep water or storm anchoring. When I set only one anchor, this would be the one.

- Alongside the primary anchor on the double anchor roller, one 33 or 44 lb. Bruce anchor (or a 35 or 45 lb. CQR) on 50 feet of 3/8" chain shackled to 200 feet of 5/8" nylon rode. All shackles should be galvanized steel (not stainless, which is too brittle), and should be safety-wired shut. I've seen some sailors use plastic wire ties as an alternative to stainless steel safety wire.

- Snubbers. Lines with chain hooks spliced on, used at anchor to take the strain of the anchor chains at the bow.

- For a stern anchor (with its own lazarette chain locker), a Danforth 22 or 35 lb. High Tensile anchor (or a 20 or 35 lb. CQR) on 25 feet of 3/8" chain and 200 feet of 1/2" line.

- For a sheet anchor (storm anchor) stowed in the bilge, a 60-80 lb. collapsible yachtsman or fisherman type anchor with 50 feet of 3/8" chain and 200 feet (or more) of rode.

You can adjust sizes to suit your vessel and brands to suit your preference, but carry at least three anchors for long-range cruising. Four is better.

Lead the heavy all-chain rode of your primary bow anchor through the divided chain locker, then as far aft and down into the bilge as possible. You can keep the bulk of the chain stored deep most of the time, leaving just what you're using on a daily basis piled in the chain locker. Before putting out to sea, rinse and dry the chain, then manually flake all of it into its deepest compartment so that only the end passes up through the chain locker to the anchor. This moves all that weight to a lower and more central center of gravity, which is better for the boat's trim and stability. I altered a bulkhead to do this on SPARROW. Some boats may benefit by installing a section of heavy PVC pipe as a conduit for leading the chain from the bottom of the chain locker to the deep storage area.

Remember to make the bitter end of all anchor rodes secure to the boat inside the chain locker (or you may find out why they call it the "bitter" end). The all-chain rode should not be shackled directly to the chain locker, but connected instead by a strong line long enough to reach the deck in case you ever need to quickly cut loose from your anchors in an emergency.

Consider installing a massive, through-bolted, back-plated padeye on the boat's stem, just above the waterline. To do this you will shackle a length of heavy nylon line eyespliced around a thimble at that end, with a chain hook secured to the other end. The line must be long enough to easily reach the foredeck. Once the anchor is set and the chain is scoped out, this line hooks to the chain, which is then fed out a little more so that the line takes the strain of the anchor. What this accomplishes is to lower the angle of pull on the anchor (as opposed to the pull coming from the height of the bow rollers, it's now coming from just above the boat's waterline), thereby reducing the amount of scope needed for a 5:1 or 7:1 scope-to-depth ratio. The line also acts as a shock absorber for the anchor chain.

Anchor rodes and dock lines should be nylon for their ability to stretch and absorb shocks. You can save money by purchasing a 600-foot spool of line from a distributor. That breaks up nicely into two 200-foot rodes plus some dock lines. Buying chain by the barrel or half-barrel is also cost effective.

A basic set of dock lines for a voyaging sailboat includes: four lines half your boat's length, four equal to your boat's length, and two twice your boat's length.

You might want to make up four chain-with-rope *mooring tails.* Eyesplice a galvanized thimble into one end of a 6- or 8-foot length of dock line. Through this eye passes a 3- to 5-foot length of hefty galvanized chain. A shackle, or more conveniently, a carabiner clip, makes the chain into a loop to secure the boat to dock fittings. The rope tail ties to your regular dock lines with a double sheet bend (not a square knot), and the dock lines are then taken up and cleated aboard. By using these tails for docking/mooring, the chain takes the abrasion off concrete piers and coarse bollards, saving much wear and tear on the dock lines (see Figure 13).

Mooring shock absorbers are useful when surge conditions put sudden, jerky strain on mooring lines at the dock. The two commonly used types, available at chandleries, are the black rubber sausage types, through which dock lines are led, and the steel spring types, which are stronger but can be noisy. As mentioned earlier, car tires can also serve this purpose admirably. Whether or not you need these aboard depends on where you're cruising.

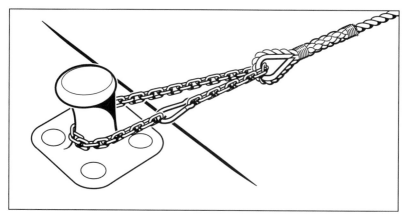

Figure 13: Rope/chain tails take the chafe of concrete piers and coarse bollards, preserving your regular dock lines.

Deck Wash Pump

I often wished I had a deck wash pump system on SPARROW during a trip up the Intracoastal Waterway on the U.S. East Coast. Every time we weighed anchor, globs of mud came aboard clinging to the chain. What a mess that made on the foredeck and in the chain locker—a real chore to clean up. How handy it would have been to simply direct a hose pumping seawater onto the chain just before it reached the bow roller.

A deck wash system will get plenty of use hosing down the chain, the decks, and the crew. A simple system consists of a 12-volt water pump mounted belowdecks, perhaps in a locker in the forward head, with an on/off switch on the foredeck. It is fed by a seawater intake hose that taps off the toilet's intake thru-hull, or any other convenient thru-hull. From the pump, a hose leads to a fitting on the foredeck to which a garden hose is attached when needed.

Jacklines

The safest way to move fore and aft along the deck of a boat under-way is with your safety harness constantly attached to the vessel. Side deck jacklines serve this purpose and they're easy to install. Just secure strong webbing (see the ORC specs in Chapter 7) between the fore-most bow deck cleat and the after-most quarterdeck cleat, or between equally sturdy fittings. Run jacklines along both the port and starboard side decks. The lines needn't be drawn very tight; just enough so it lies easily on the deck. When you're in the cockpit offshore, you can clip your harness to the windward jackline, so you're ready to scoot forward quickly if necessary. Jacklines can also be made up of coated wire or a 3/8" or 1/2" line. However, unlike webbing, these may roll underfoot when stepped on, which is dangerous on a pitching deck. Jacklines are removed and stowed when in port.

Steering

Aboard a well-balanced sailboat less than 40 feet, wheel vs. tiller steer-ing should be a matter of personal inclination. Some boats, however, require more mechanical advantage than others to control the rudder, either by virtue of the rudder's size or by accident of design. Even after you've done everything possible to improve balance and trim, you may still need a wheel to achieve tireless steering. Thankfully, SPARROW was not one of those, and by choice I enjoyed the simplicity, the directness, and the increased cockpit space that tiller steering provides. Whether you steer by tiller or by wheel, carry an emergency tiller that can be quickly fitted if the primary means of steering breaks. The emergency tiller should be usable without having to open a hatch, as is the case in some yacht designs.

Wheel steering systems, even worm screw gears, require regular inspection and lubrication. Carry spare cables, clamps, sprocket chain (if used), and pulleys for a cable steering system, or spare parts and fluid for a hydraulic system.

During your next haul out, consider drilling a 3/4" hole in the rudder, near the aft top corner. Bevel the rims, seal the inside surface with a coating of epoxy, and sand the hole smooth. If the ship's steering system ever fails and cannot be operated from the deck, this hole can be used to attach lines that are led to the cockpit winches for direct, emergency steering.

Self-Steering

Self-steering is the greatest boon to ocean voyaging since the fore and aft rig replaced square sails. Don't leave port without it. There are two popular types of self-steering today, the windvane and the autopilot.

A windvane, which steers a course relative to wind direction, generally responds quicker in rough conditions than does an autopilot, uses no electricity, and is quiet. It is particularly useful when beating against a shifting wind, because it will keep the boat headed at the optimum angle as the wind backs or veers. Running before the wind, the vane reduces the risk of jibing by again following changes in wind direction. Of course, windvanes steer well on reaches, too, when the ability to follow variable winds isn't so critical. I've sailed tens of thousands of miles with a Monitor windvane. With its all stainless steel construction and intelligent engineering, it is a reliable, tireless crew offshore.

On the down side, a good, manufactured windvane is expensive and is vulnerable to damage and theft hanging out off the transom. Its greatest drawback, however, is that it doesn't work when motoring.

The electronic autopilot, on the other hand, steers a boat under power or sail. It steers a compass course that you set, but some models can optionally interface with a wind direction sensor in order to steer a course by the wind instead, which is sometimes desirable as just mentioned. For these reasons, if I had to choose between just having a windvane and just having an autopilot, I'd choose the latter—though I prefer to carry both. Consider the autopilot to be essential equipment and pack a spare unit if you can afford it, or at least a very complete repair and rebuild kit including a spare drive motor.

Most of today's autopilots use a modest amount of electricity and steer well, but some are clearly engineered and built better than others. I don't want to tell you which one to buy, because marine electronics change constantly and you need to have the latest information to make an informed decision. This is a subject best covered by boating magazines, and they do it often and well. I suggest you educate yourself before choosing an autopilot by reading the latest articles comparing popular brands, talking to other sailors on the docks and online chat groups, and generally researching what's working best today. The most advertised brand is not necessarily the best choice.

I was able to flip SPARROW's tiller over the lazarette so that it pointed backwards, and I wound up connecting both the external autopilot and the windvane back there, in the reversed position (see Figure 14). This left the cockpit entirely clear of tiller and steering apparatus offshore, making it a much more accommodating living space. Still, I could instantly disconnect the self-steering and flip the tiller forward to return to manual steering. The ability to open up the cockpit space in this way is, in my opinion, a strong point in favor of tiller steering on small to mid-size cruising sailboats.

It is difficult to overemphasize the value of self-steering to the short-handed and singlehanded sailor. When (when, not if) your primary systems fail in mid-ocean, a solution will be as precious to you as the proverbial glass of water in the desert. For a last ditch, back-up self-steering system, see if you can find either of these books: *Self-Steering for Sailing Craft* by John S. Letcher, Jr. or *Self-Steering Without a Windvane* by Lee Woas. Both offer detailed explanations of the sheet-to-tiller system of self-steering, which requires little more than some small blocks, shock cord and patience to assemble. Unfortunately, both books are out of print, but you can occasionally find used copies. I tested this system myself on a sail from St. Petersburg to Key West, Florida. It definitely works, although it's a chore to set up and adjust and so is practical only as an emergency back-up system to an autopilot and/or a windvane. Try using it before you need it to be sure you have the necessary pieces, then stow it away as emergency gear. You just might bless your foresight someday.

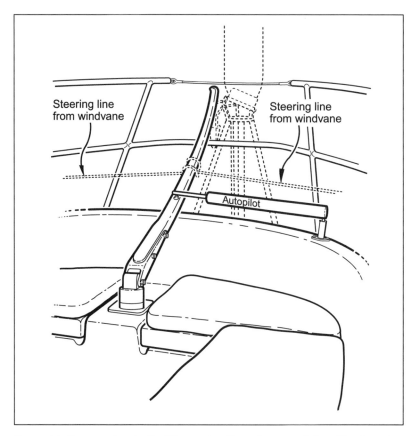

Figure 14: On some boats, the tiller can be flipped over and aimed backwards, leaving the cockpit wide open while either the windvane or the autopilot steers from the afterdeck.

Compass

The ship's primary navigational compass is a vital piece of equipment. You generally get what you pay for, and this is not a good place to skimp. Choose one with large, easy to read numbers. A red compass night light is necessary and usually built in. You might want to install a dimmer switch to tone down the light on dark night watches.

Learn to swing and correct the compass yourself from a seamanship book such as Chapman's *Piloting, Seamanship, and Small Boat*

Handling This will enable you to make and update the compass deviation card that you'll need to navigate accurately.

Mounting a small compass belowdecks, readable from your sea berth, makes it easy to check the boat's heading during off-watch rest periods. There are compasses specially designed to be mounted overhead. You can read them while lying in your bunk.

In addition, carry at least one other compass aboard so you won't be in bad trouble if a flying winch handle shatters the primary unit. In a pinch, a good hand-bearing compass can serve as an emergency back-up navigational compass. Some higher end binoculars offer a compass read through the lenses—a handy tool in general, and another back-up compass for emergency use.

Cockpit Table

Dining topside is a delight in mild weather. A table in the cockpit facilitates this. If you have pedestal wheel steering, there are prefabricated tables made to collapse against the pedestal for easy storage. A tiller in the down position can support a custom made table that clamps onto it. Alternatively, an ordinary small card table with folding legs may serve admirably, or you can fabricate your own with a few raw materials.

Cockpit Cushions

Closed cell foam is the modern way to go when ordering new cockpit cushions. It doesn't absorb water so the cushions dry quickly. Closed cell foam floats and can double as a swim cushion. Consult your canvas shop about cover fabrics. Synthetics that don't hold water are best, and light colors won't burn your buns when you sit down on a hot, sunny day. If one side of the cockpit cushions is covered with a vinyl mesh, it will allow the cushion surface to drain and air out. For good looks, the canvas shop can trim your cushion covers with piping that matches the boat's color scheme. Be sure any zippers in the covers are entirely plastic, including the zipper cars and pull-tabs.

Non-Skid

If the builder of your boat left any slick deck surfaces wider than an inch or two, I suggest you non-skid them. They're as dangerous as a banana peel. At the boarding gates, non-skid the cap rail if it's a slippery surface such as varnished wood. I like the prefabricated rubberized or polymer tread non-skid material you cut to shape and glue on, but deck paint with garnet or quartz silica sand in it works great, too. If you're painting or re-painting an entire deck using sand for non-skid, you can purchase a 50- or 100-lb. bag of even-sized silica sand from a foundry supplier who sells it as casting sand, or from a sand-blasting facility. It's much more economical than buying the little cans of sand sold at marine stores. Use a flour sifter to spread it evenly onto a wet coat of paint and then, after it dries, put a cover coat over it.

Exterior Wood Trim (Brightwork)

Some teak trim above decks can be attractive; too much becomes a real maintenance chore. I know I'm risking being hung for heresy by brightwork aficionados, but if your boat is over-teaked, you might consider painting some of it. However, lay a few coats of varnish over the wood first, so that the paint doesn't get into the grain and can be stripped off in the future if you, or a future owner, choose to return to the natural wood finish.

Techniques for the care and feeding of teak are not within the scope of this book; whether you varnish, oil, paint or go natural is a matter of personal preference. However, any teak that is going to be stepped upon (like decks and coamings) or grabbed (like handrails) should not be varnished. A varnished surface, when wet with water, is very slippery and very dangerous.

Swim Ladder

Ah, to greet the sunrise in a deserted tropical lagoon. You step naked into the balmy morning air and while the coffee is percolating belowdecks, dive overboard into the warm, crystalline water. Heaven on earth!

Swimming off the boat is one of the great joys of warm weather cruising, and you'll need a way to climb back aboard. A permanently mounted, swing-up ladder aft will get plenty of use, and is preferable to the foldable ones you dig out from under coils of line and garden hose in the lazarette.

Whatever you normally use to climb out of the water, plan a way to get yourself back on deck if you go overboard with no ladder lowered and no one to assist. If your boat has a swing-down ladder, attach a lanyard that hangs within easy reach of a swimmer and will, if tugged, lower the ladder for boarding. A windvane mount can provide adequate foot- and handholds for climbing aboard, but it's usually a bit too high for the average person to scramble up from the water. You might add a lower rung to that mount that a swimmer can pull down into the water for the first step. Small steps/handholds permanently mounted on the transom work well on some boats. Whatever your set-up, provide some permanent means of getting out of the water. Don't ignore this minor safety feature. There's a reasonable chance that someone will need it someday, and its absence could suddenly become a serious matter.

Chapter 6

~~

The Hull

Hull Color

L. Francis Herreshoff once said, "There are only two colors to paint a boat: white or black—and only a fool would paint it black."

Well, I've been called worse. Personally, I think a colored hull, other than white, can accent the pretty sheer of a vessel, assuming she has one. However, keep in mind that a dark colored hull will get hotter in tropical climates where keeping cool below is a worthy goal. Also, dark gel coat colors fade and chalk in the sun long before light or white hulls. A wooden hull painted a dark color may encourage rot by absorbing more of the sun's heat. If you're planning long spells in warm places, choose a light colored hull. Cream, beige, ivory, or a pastel color, with complimentary darker boot and sheer stripes, are attractive alternatives to plain old white or black. Of course, any color other than white on the decks will get too hot to walk on barefoot.

Rubrails and Fender Boards

Make sure your boat's rubrails – the rails that run along both sides of the hull a foot or two below the sheer—are hefty, protruding well beyond the outboard edge of the cap rails. If your boat doesn't have rubrails, you might want to add them. We all have our days when the docking maneuver just doesn't go as planned, and a substantial rubrail will protect the hull from our little shortcomings. A wood rubrail should be capped with stainless steel half-round.

When docked against a piling or other protrusion, a fender board gives broader protection to the hull than a plain fender, which might be pushed out of place. The simplest fender board is made from a 4- to 10-ft., 2x6 wood plank with a pair of holes drilled near each end for attaching the lines that hang it over the side. It is positioned perpendicular to the piling or dock against which it lies. Two or three fenders are hung between the board and the hull. If you can afford the storage space, two short (vertical) and two long (horizontal) fender boards should suffice for most occasions.

Thru-Hull Fittings

Any hole in the bottom of my boat makes me nervous, even the intentional ones, so I'm fussy about the thru-hulls. Below the water line, these fittings should be proper bronze seacocks, isolated when installed in metal hulls. Gate valves are unacceptable—they corrode and seize up. Don't forget to lubricate the seacocks periodically, since their smooth operation may become urgently important at any time.

Be sure you have a tapered wooden plug made up to fit each thru-hull pipe. Each plug should be tied or otherwise secured near to its seacock, inside, so that if you suddenly need to stopper a fitting, you'll know where to find the correct plug instantly. Put a label or tag on each thru-hull identifying its function. Make a diagram of all the boat's thru-hull locations and keep it handy for quick reference in case you suddenly find the bilges full of seawater and need to locate all possible sources of the leak.

Stuffing Boxes

The stuffing box seals the perimeter of the propeller shaft where it passes through the hull, to prevent seawater from entering the boat around the shaft. A leaking stuffing box is one of the most common sources of seawater entering a yacht and is usually the first place to check when you find the water level rising in the bilges. The stuffing box works by compressing the flax packing by tightening down on a large cap nut. This packing nut, once adjusted correctly, is held securely in place by a lock nut. You need to have two wrenches aboard big enough to fit over each of these nuts in order to adjust and service the stuffing box.

If you don't know the last time your stuffing box was re-packed and the boat is more than a few years old, go ahead and replace the packing now, before you venture offshore. This is done most easily while the boat is in dry-dock or careened, but can be done in the water if you know what you're doing. Lots of water will enter the boat while you're re-packing the tube in the water, but your bilge pumps should be able to handle it for the five minutes or so it takes. New packing will require you to tighten the stuffing box after each use for a while until the packing is set, but it will then last a long time with only slight, periodic tightening. The rule of thumb is to tighten the packing nut while the shaft is spinning, just enough so that a drop or two of seawater drips into the bilge through the stuffing box every 30 to 60 seconds when the shaft is turning. If the packing is over-tightened so that no water enters at all when motoring, the shaft is not being sufficiently cooled at the packing. This will overheat the shaft and the packing, and may score the shaft permanently. If the packing is not tight enough, water will drip into the boat even when the shaft is not turning. It's not hard to set it just right, but remember to check and adjust it periodically.

Carry enough extra packing for at least one replacement—a 2-foot length should be ample. Packing is not expensive. I recommend using the new Teflon flax packing, which creates less friction, less heat, lower wear and a tighter fit. A handy tool for removing the old packing is a flax packing extractor—kind of like a long, thin corkscrew designed to reach in between the shaft and the packing gland and snag the packing to draw it out. A good chandlery will sell them.

A neat way to eliminate the whole stuffing box maintenance and adjustment routine is to replace it with one of the more modern shaft seal systems such as the Last-Drop brand or PYI's Packless Sealing System. These create a mechanical seal around the shaft by means of a high-density carbon-graphite and stainless steel flange attached by a rubber bellows-like hose section. The Last-Drop unit on SPARROW performed flawlessly for 30,000 nautical miles, never needing attention.

Cutless Bearing

The cutless bearing is a bronze tube fabricated with a longitudinally grooved rubber liner. It fits into the hull's stern tube and the supporting strut, if there is one, through which the propeller shaft passes. It is the bearing surface on which the shaft rides. The rubber liner of the cutless bearing will eventually wear out with use, sooner if the engine alignment is off. You can check your boat's cutless bearing by firmly grasping the shaft just outside of the hull, and trying to jerk it up and down. If it wobbles, that indicates a worn bearing. The point at which the wobble indicates the need to replace the cutless bearing is a matter of feel. The first time you're checking this, ask the boatyard manager or a marine mechanic for their opinion.

Changing the cutless bearing generally requires that you first remove the prop shaft. Then check for and loosen any set screws that secure the cutless bearing in place (they're usually Allen-head screws set flush with the outside of the stern tube, and are often hidden by several coats of bottom paint). Then you can pound out the old cutless bearing from inside the hull using a piece of pipe or wooden dowel of the correct diameter. Finally, tap the new bearing into place from the outside using a block of wood between the end of the bearing and the hammer to avoid damaging the bronze tube. Re-tighten the set screws and put the shaft back in.

Blisters

Gelcoat-covered fiberglass is not entirely waterproof and will absorb water over time. This can eventually lead to osmotic blistering, the formation of bubbles in the hull's surface, usually below the waterline. It's not at all uncommon for fiberglass boats to develop a few blisters from time to time. These can be repaired in dry-dock by gouging them out, letting the fiberglass dry thoroughly, and refilling the voids with epoxy or with vinylester resin. In rare cases, the blistering can become so pronounced that it compromises the integrity of the fiberglass laminates. It may then become necessary to peel away the outer layer of the hull using a special grinding tool for that purpose, and then apply layers of epoxy or vinylester resin. If your boat has a serious blister problem, consult a boatyard experienced in blister treatment and repair, or educate yourself on the latest do-it-yourself procedures.

The best preventive treatment for osmotic blistering on fiberglass boat hulls is to seal the boat's bottom before blisters get started. Some experts recommend applying coats of epoxy. Others believe vinylester resin is more impervious to water and longer lasting. Most boatyards can do the job for you, but if you're an inveterate do-it-yourselfer, or just working within a tight budget, the application process is not difficult. It may require the boat to sit out of the water for weeks or even months to let the fiberglass dry out first, depending on the moisture content of the hull. If you're coating the hull, it doesn't hurt to coat the aluminum propane tanks at the same time, if they're unpainted. If possible, also coat any metal tanks in the boat that are accessible. Their welds are vulnerable to electrolytic corrosion that can eventually result in leaks, especially if the bottom of the tank rests in or near the bilge where salt water can get at it. If you're having a brand new boat built, have the manufacturer seal the boat's bottom and any tanks that sit in or nearly in the bilge.

The Dinghy

Behold the little giant, carting people and provisions to and from shore, battling to windward in a blow, exploring distant reefs and landing on rugged shores. The cruising dinghy has got its work cut out. Like the mother ship, the dink needs to be tough and versatile.

Cruisers are faced with the choice between a hard dinghy and an inflatable, and as always there are pros and cons to both. The hard dinghy rows better, is handier for carrying out an anchor with chain and rode, can be rigged to sail (which is a fun way to explore harbors), and virtually never wears out. But it can be cumbersome to stow on deck for offshore passages, slow under power and relatively unstable in general.

On the other hand, the inflatable is wonderfully stable even for scuba diving expeditions and most stow away in a locker. Best of all, if the model features rigid floorboards, it can be very fast under power, expanding the range of exploration and making trips ashore a snap. But it doesn't row worth a darn in a blow, so you more or less need an outboard motor and all the paraphernalia that goes with that, including highly flammable gasoline. Also, inflatables all spring leaks eventually, requiring more and more patching as they age and wear. A popular hybrid is the hard-bottomed inflatable. It is fast and stable and can take a rough grounding, but it does not stow away as easily as a soft-bottomed boat.

If you can afford it, one option is to carry one of each, which not only gives you the advantages (and, alas, the disadvantages) of both, but also makes you a two-dinghy family. This enables you and your mate to come and go separately when living at anchor. That was the solution aboard SPARROW—a Trinka sailing dinghy named TAILFEATHER, and a small Avon inflatable we called RUBBERDUCK, with a modest, 3-HP outboard motor. A bigger inflatable and more powerful outboard will vastly increase your excursion range when the mother ship is anchored. If your boat is big enough to accommodate that, it's probably worth it.

Here's what you should carry aboard your dinghy: registration, PFDs for each passenger, oars, anchor, rode, bailer and sponge, flashlight, basic engine spares (cord, spark plug, sheer pin tools) and a lock with cable or chain to secure the boat and the motor at docks.

In states and countries that require it, a motor driven dinghy must have registration numbers and stickers showing. It's a good idea to label dinghies with your own name, radio call sign or monitored VHF channel, and a telephone number and/or e-mail address. There are lots of honest people in this world who would return a found dinghy should yours ever drift away, so make it easy for them. However, if you identify the dinghy's mother ship by name, thieves can readily identify which boat out in the harbor is unguarded while you're ashore. So I would advise you to avoid labeling your dink with "Tender To (vessel's name)."

Dinghy davits on the stern of your boat make dinghy storage and launching a cinch, although in really big, breaking following seas this arrangement might be dangerous. It's good practice to stow the dinghy on deck, rather than in davits, for offshore passages.

A sailboard, once you get the hang of it, makes a great extra dinghy and a fun toy, too. I've seen one or two small-boat cruisers that use a sailboard as their sole tender.

I have long thought that there is a need for a practical lifeboat aboard offshore cruising sailboats. Of course, most boats simply aren't big enough to carry a proper lifeboat as we think of them. Still, an inflatable or an unsinkable hard dinghy could potentially serve that purpose. To be sure, a well designed liferaft will fare better in severe weather conditions, and I'd advise you to carry one on board your boat. However, a lifeboat with a reefable sailing rig offers castaways the opportunity to progress toward safety or rescue, rather than drifting around helplessly waiting for someone to find them. This is a worthwhile consideration for any offshore sailor.

If you can figure out a way to carry a dinghy/lifeboat, it should have the sailing rig and the survival gear (see the Abandon Ship Survival Kit list in Chapter 8) stored aboard when it's cradled on deck or in davits, and it would need to be decked over by a supported canvas cover with a zipper or Velcro opening for quick entry. If your yacht's lifeboat/tender is big enough, consider storing the liferaft inside of it during passages. This increases your chances of escaping quickly with both in an emergency, giving you the option to use either or both as the situation demands. It is possible to tow a liferaft with a sailing dinghy, at least to the extent of directing a course off the wind.

There is an inflatable dinghy on the market called the Tinker that seems to answer this need for a tender, a liferaft and a lifeboat aboard the cruising yacht. Made in England, the Tinker combines an inflatable dinghy that can be rowed or motored, with an optional, collapsible, reefable sailing rig and an optional survival canopy for quick conversion into a liferaft. Such a craft must inevitably compromise some attributes compared to products dedicated to just rowing or motoring or sailing or surviving. Nevertheless, it is the only manufactured boat of which I am aware that even attempts to combine all of these features into a single, well-made vessel. The only obvious downside to the Tinker is its price, which is in the $3,500 to $5,000 range, depending on size, by the time you order all the options. Sizes available are 9', 10'3" and 12'.

Chapter 7

Safety Afloat

Safety must be a primary consideration aboard every vessel. The unique environment of a boat, combined with the unforgiving nature of the sea, requires special equipment and rules and a degree of vigilance unequalled in most other endeavors. Throughout the book, I express my own ideas on safety aspects of outfitting a cruising sailboat. They generally agree in practice, though not always in detail, with the official rules.

In this chapter, I quote selectively and without comment from published safety regulations of several leading authorities: the Offshore Racing Council (ORC) Special Regulations Governing Offshore Racing, with insertions from The Whitbread Round The World Race (Whitbread) ORC Special Regulations and Amendments, and the United States Coast Guard (USCG) Federal Requirements for Recreational Boats. I've selected only those points that I feel are most applicable to us cruisers, and which may not be covered adequately in the other chapters.

It is both prudent and wise for mariners to be thoroughly familiar with all safety precautions pertaining to boating and the sea. I encourage you to obtain the above and similar publications, and read them in their entirety. Particularly, the International Convention for the Safety of Life at Sea (SOLAS) defines safety procedures and equipment of the highest standards. In addition, *Cruising World* magazine sponsors instructive Safety At Sea seminars, announced regularly in the magazine.

ORC Regulations

2.0   *Owner's Responsibility*

2.1   The safety of the yacht and her crew is the sole and inescapable responsibility of the owner or owner's representative, who must do his/her best to ensure that the yacht is fully found, thoroughly seaworthy and manned by an experienced crew who are physically fit to face bad weather. He must be satisfied as to the soundness of hull, spars, rigging, sails and all gear. He must ensure that all safety equipment is properly maintained and stowed and that the crew knows where it is kept and how it is to be used.

4.0   *Categories of Offshore Events*

4.2   Category 0 race. Trans-Ocean races, where yachts must be completely self-sufficient for very extended periods of time, capable of withstanding heavy storms and prepared to meet serious emergencies without the expectation of outside assistance.

5.0   *Basic Requirements*

5.1   All required equipment shall: Function properly. Be readily accessible. Be of a type, size and capacity suitable and adequate for the intended use and size of the yacht.

5.2   Yachts shall be self-righting (see I.O.R. Part XII). They shall be strongly built, watertight and, particularly with regard to hulls, decks and cabin trunks, capable of withstanding solid water and knockdowns. They must be properly rigged and ballasted, be fully seaworthy and must meet the standards set forth herein. "Properly rigged" means (inter alia) that shrouds shall never be disconnected.

5.3   Inboard engine installations shall be such that the engine when running can be securely covered, and that the exhaust and fuel supply systems are securely installed and adequately protected from the effects of heavy weather. When an electric starter is the only provision for starting the engine, a separate battery shall be carried, the primary purpose of which is to start the engine.

5.4   Ballast and Heavy Equipment. All heavy items including inside ballast and internal fittings (such as batteries, stoves, gas bottles, tanks, engines, outboard motors, etc.) and anchors and chains (see 8.31 and 8.32) shall be securely fastened so as to remain in position should the yacht be capsized 180 degrees.

6.0   *Structural Features*

6.12   Hatches. . . . The companionway hatch shall be fitted with a strong securing arrangement which shall be operable from above and below.

6.13   Companionways. All blocking arrangements (washboards, hatch-boards, etc.) shall be capable of being secured in position with the hatch open or shut and shall be secured to the yacht by lanyard or other mechanical means to prevent their being lost overboard.

6.21   Cockpits shall be . . . self-draining.

6.31   Cockpit drains. Cockpit drains adequate to drain cockpits quickly but with a combined area (after allowance for screens, if attached) of not less than the equivalent of four 0.75 in. (19mm) diameter drains. . . . Cockpits shall drain at all angles of heel.

6.52   Soft wood plugs, tapered and of the correct size, to be attached to, or adjacent to, the appropriate (thru-hull) fitting.

6.54   The heel of a keel-stepped mast shall be securely fastened to the mast step or adjoining structure.

6.55   Bulkhead. The hull shall have a watertight bulkhead within 15% of the vessel's length from the bow and abaft the forward perpendicular.
(Whitbread Amendment): . . . any openings therein shall be capable of withstanding flood water to their full height plus 50% from either side. Openings shall be capable of rapid closing at all times.

6.61.1   Lifeline Enclosure Material.
All lifelines shall be stranded stainless steel wire of the

minimum diameter as given below. Grade 316 stainless wire is recommended.

Length Overall	*Min. Diameter*
Under 28.0 ft. (8.53m)	1/8" (3 mm)
28.0 ft. (8.53m) to 43.0 ft. (13.0m) inclusive	5/32" (4 mm)
Over 43.0 ft. (13.0m)	3/16" (5 mm)

. . . All wire, fittings, anchor point fixtures and any lanyards shall comprise a lifeline enclosure system such that the entire enclosure is at all points of at least the breaking strength of the required lifeline wire.

6.61.4 . . . Pulpits and stanchions shall be securely attached . . . thru-bolted, bonded or welded . . .

6.62.1 Taut double lifelines, with upper lifeline at a height of not less than 2 ft. (609 mm) above the working deck, to be permanently supported (by stanchions, etc.) at intervals of not more that 7 ft. (2.13m).

6.65 Jackstays. Jackstays must be fitted on deck, port and starboard of the yacht's centerline to provide secure attachments for safety harnesses. Jackstays shall comprise stainless steel 1x19 wire of minimum diameter 5 mm, or webbing of equivalent strength. Jackstays must be attached to through-bolted or welded deck plates, or other suitable and strong anchorages. The jackstays must, if possible, be fitted in such a way that a crewmember, when clipped on, can move from a cockpit to the forward and to the after end of the main deck without unclipping the harness. If the deck layout renders this impossible, additional lines must be fitted so that a crewmember can move as described with a minimum of clipping operations.

A crewmember must be able to clip on before coming on deck, unclip after going below and remain clipped on while moving laterally across the yacht on the foredeck, the afterdeck, and amidships. If necessary, additional jackstays and/or through-bolted or welded anchorage points must be provided for this purpose.

Through-bolted or welded anchorage points, or other suitable and strong anchorage, for safety harnesses must be provided adjacent to stations such as the helm, sheet winches and masts, where crewmembers work for long periods. Jack-stays should be sited in such a way that the safety harness lanyard can be kept as short as possible.

7.0	*Accommodations*
7.3	Cooking stove, securely installed against a capsize with safe accessible fuel shut-off control capable of being safely operated in a seaway.
7.55	(Whitbread Amendment) Adequate arrangement shall be available for the collection of rain water and/or for distilling or desalinating sea water. A minimum of 4 hand desalination units shall be carried, any 50% of which shall be capable of desalinating 4 pints (2.3 liters) per competitor per day.
8.0	*General Equipment*
8.1	Fire extinguishers, at least two, readily accessible in suitable and different parts of the boat.

USCG Classification of Fire Extinguishers

Classification (type size)	B-I	B-II
Foam (minimum gallons)	1 1/4	2 1/2
Carbon Dioxide (minimum lbs.)	4	15
Dry Chemical (minimum lbs.)	2	10
Halon (minimum lbs.)	2 1/2	10

USCG Minimum Number of Hand Portable Fire Extinguishers Required

Vessel Length	No Fixed System	With Approved Fixed System
Less than 26'	1 B-I	0
26' to less than 40'	2 B-I or 1 B-II	1 B-I
40' to 65'	3 B-I or 1 B-II	2 B-I or 1 B-II and 1 B-I

8.2   (Whitbread Amendment) Fire blankets. At least one, to be stowed close to the galley ready for immediate use.

USCG Sound Signaling Devices

(Vessels less than 12 meters) . . . must have some means of making an efficient sound signal. Vessels 12 meters or more in length are required to carry on board a power whistle or power horn and a bell.

8.21.1   Bilge Pumps, at least two manually operated, securely fitted to the yacht's structure, one operable above, the other below deck. Each pump shall be operable with all cockpit seats, hatches and companionways shut.

8.21.2   Each bilge pump shall be provided with permanently fitted discharge pipe(s) of sufficient capacity to accommodate simultaneously both pumps.

8.41   (Whitbread Amendment) Flashlights, at least three, one of which is suitable for signaling, water resistant, with spare batteries and bulbs.

8.51   (Whitbread Amendment). . . . Crewmembers shall be trained to the following levels:

   a. Hold a recognized, current (within 2 years), national first aid certificate including cardiopulmonary resuscitation.

   b. Apply simple strapping and plaster casts.

   c. Be able to undertake skin suturing.

   d. Insert intravenous cannulae and give intravenous fluids.

e. Give both intramuscular and intravenous injections.

f. Receive instruction in endotracheal intubation and cricothyrotomy.

g. Receive instruction in temporary dental fillings.

8.55 (Whitbread Amendment) The World Health Organization International Medical Guide for Ships (2nd Edition) . . . shall be carried for use as a common reference when radio medical advice is sought.

8.56 (Whitbread Amendment) Crew medicals. All crewmembers shall undergo a medical examination . . . (prior to departure)

10.0 *Emergency Equipment*

10.5 Yacht's name on miscellaneous buoyant equipment, such as life jackets, oars, cushions, life buoys and lifeslings, etc.

10.51 Life buoys, lifeslings, liferafts, and life jackets shall be fitted with marine grade retro-reflective material.

10.61 Marine radio transmitter and receiver. If the regular antenna depends upon the mast, an emergency antenna must be provided.

11.0 *Safety Equipment*

11.1 Life jackets, one for each crewmember. "A life jacket should be of a form which is capable of providing not less than 16 kg. of buoyancy, arranged so that an unconscious man will be securely suspended face upwards at approximately 45 degrees to the water surface."

11.1 (Whitbread Amendment) Life jackets, one for each crewmember plus one spare. All shall be inflatable and . . . be fitted with a crotch strap . . . (and) shall be fitted for fully automatic inflation. . . .

(USCG) A Type I PFD, or Offshore Life Jacket . . . is effective for all waters, especially open, rough or remote waters where rescue may be delayed. It is designed to turn most unconscious wearers in the water to a face-up position. Type I comes in two sizes. The adult size provides at least 22 pounds buoyancy, the child size, 11 pounds, minimum.

11.2 Whistles attached to life jackets.

11.3 (Whitbread Amendment) Note: All fatalities in previous WRTW Races resulted from man overboard incidents. The diligent use of a properly adjusted safety harness is regarded as by far the most effective way of preventing man overboard incidents.

11.4 D. Each (life) raft shall be capable of being got to the lifelines within 15 seconds. (Whitbread Amendment to 11.4) They must . . . have been inspected and tested within a year preceding the finish of the Race.

11.41.2 (Whitbread Amendment) Hand desalination units to provide sufficient fresh water for the full raft capacity and rations shall be carried . . . to accompany rafts in waterproof, buoyant grab bags. . . .

11.51 Life buoy with a drogue, or lifesling, equipped with a self-igniting light within reach of the helmsman and ready for instant use.

11.52 In addition to 11.51. One life buoy, within reach of the helmsman and ready for instant use and equipped with a whistle, dye marker, drogue, a self-igniting light, and a pole and flag. The pole shall be either permanently extended or be capable of being fully automatically extended in less than 20 seconds. It shall be attached to the life buoy with 10-ft. (3.048m) of floating line and is to be of a length and so ballasted that the flag will fly at least 6 ft. (1.828m) off the water.

11.61 Distress signals conforming to the current International Convention for the Safety of Life at Sea (SOLAS) regulations (chapter III Visual Signals) to be stowed in a waterproof container or containers, as indicated.

11.62 Twelve red parachute flares (SOLAS regulation 35).

11.63 Four white parachute flares (SOLAS regulation 35).

11.64 Four red hand flares (SOLAS regulation 36).

11.65 Four white hand flares. Although not specified by SOLAS, it is recommended that design criteria, excepting colour and candela rating, be in accordance with SOLAS regulation 36.

11.66 Two orange smoke day signals (SOLAS regulation 37).

11.67 Distress signals which are more than 3 years old (as indicated by the date of manufacture) or of which the date of expiry has passed are not acceptable.

11.7 Heaving line (50 ft. (15.24m) minimum length) readily accessible to cockpit.

Chapter 8

⌒⌒

Prepare to Survive

Safety equipment in general, and emergency survival equipment in particular, sometimes get less serious attention than they deserve. The "it won't happen to me" syndrome is a malady that afflicts us all to some extent, but the only effective way to prepare for worst case scenarios, like abandoning ship at sea, is to treat it as something that actually will occur. If you take the attitude that you definitely will need and use this equipment someday, you're likely to do a much better job of preparing yourself, your crew, and your vessel for disaster. "Hope for the best, but prepare for the worst" is our motto.

To help you get into the right thinking mode for this, you ought to read one of the several, true survival stories found on marine store bookshelves. *Adrift* by Steven Callahan is an excellent choice, as are *Survivor* by Michael Greenwald and the classic *117 Days Adrift* by Maurice and Maralyn Bailey.

Liferaft

I've never liked the idea of tying up so much money in something I hope never to use, but the alternative is unthinkable. So I invested in a Givens six-man canister liferaft. It nestled on deck in its own stainless steel mounting cradle. Originally, the liferaft was installed on top of the coach house just forward of the mast, as so many of them are on yachts. But it blocked the helmsman's view ahead from the cockpit. So I remounted it on the sloped forward end of the cabin trunk. Ideally, if there's room in or around your cockpit, that would be a better location for a liferaft, at least when sailing offshore. If, instead of a canister-packed liferaft, you have a liferaft packed in a soft valise case, it ought to be stored out of the weather but instantly available, such as in a cockpit locker with nothing stored on top of it.

The liferaft needs a quick way of releasing from its stored position. There are hydrostatic releases available that will release the raft automatically from a sinking vessel, in case you don't have time to do it manually. The liferaft should have its painter attached to the boat so that it won't blow away when inflated, with a knife in a handy sheath to sever the line when ready. Some liferaft painters have an intentional "weak link" that will part from a sinking vessel. However, once in the raft, don't cut it free until the ship actually submerges. According to Captain Ron Trossbach, former Director of U.S. Navy Sailing, it is better to stay near a semi-submerged boat because it is often found by search teams before the raft. Also, when things settle down, you may be able to salvage more supplies from the mother ship.

A liferaft should include a pair of paddles (oars for a lifeboat). Life jackets should be on board, plus at least one life jacket tied to the survival kit to give it extra flotation.

The Abandon Ship Survival Kit

Several years ago, while delivering a boat to the Virgin Islands, I responded to a distress call and rescued six castaways from a tiny, half swamped dory in mid-ocean. They had been unprepared to abandon ship, and yet had been forced to by a sudden, uncontrollable electrical fire aboard their 108-foot commercial fishing vessel. These men would almost certainly have perished at sea had we not come to their aid.

Most obviously lacking aboard their lifeboat was a survival kit, a bag of gear pre-packed and instantly ready to go into the survival craft. With the right equipment and a positive mental attitude, castaways can survive for months at sea if need be. Prepare an *abandon ship survival kit* to be carried aboard your boat, and drill your crew in advance with a procedure for leaving the vessel in an emergency.

A hand-operated water desalinator watermaker is a number one priority item for survival at sea in a liferaft. The Pur Survivor 06, compact in size and weighing only 2.5 lbs., makes an ounce of drinking water in less than 2 minutes (nearly 2 pints per hour). It belongs in every liferaft and/or survival kit, along with its instruction manual in a sealed plastic bag.

Should you have to abandon ship, the completeness of the survival kit you take with you could mean the difference between life and death. Pack your survival gear in a heavy-duty plastic river-rafting bag or strong duffel bag and store the bag, together with two 5-gallon jugs of water, in a readily accessible location, such as in a cockpit locker. Tie a brass or plastic whistle and a small, waterproof strobe light to the outside of the bag. The pack and water jugs should float—fasten a life preserver to the pack and leave some air in the jugs. Attach to each of them 30 feet of line as lanyards. Be sure to use brightly colored polypropylene line because it floats and is easily seen. Just before each offshore passage, refill the water jugs with fresh water and inspect and upgrade the entire survival kit. Upon launching the liferaft or lifeboat in an emergency, the survival kit bag and the water jugs should immediately be tied to the survival craft or stored inside.

Abandon Ship Survival Kit List

Packed loosely in a bag:

- 1 hand operated water desalinator

- 2 compact solar stills

- SOLAS grade flares: 6 hand-launched parachute, 6 handheld red, 4 handheld white, 2 orange smoke, 1 flare-launching pistol with 12 red parachute and 6 red meteor flares

- Sea dye markers

- Collapsible 10-inch radar reflector and/or parafoil kite reflector
- 1 gallon jug of water
- 2 1-gallon foldable water jugs
- 6-foot square piece of Dacron cloth (multi-use)
- 1 square foot 1/4-inch plywood for a cutting board
- Raft patching kit
- Raft pump plus one spare pump (or repair parts)
- Hand bearing compass
- Sea anchor
- Fishing trident and broom handle
- Folding fishing rod
- Double-banded spear gun with extra stainless steel tips
- Fish gaff (with point well protected)
- Swim goggles or dive mask
- Clean sponge (for collecting condensation)
- 2 light rain suits
- Sea soap
- Two sprouting jars (for sprouting seeds and beans)

Tightly sealed in plastic containers:

- 20 packages and cans of food
- 12 high-energy food bars
- Large container of honey

- Large, sealed bag of dried fruit
- 1 bottle multi-vitamin pills including vitamin C
- Assorted seeds and beans for sprouting (mung, alfalfa, etc.)
- Small can opener
- 2 spoons, 2 forks
- 2 butane lighters and several books of waterproof matches
- Small medical (first aid) kit
- 2 rolls surgical gauze
- Seasickness pills
- Large tube #30 sun-block cream
- E.P.I.R.B. (406 MHz)
- Handheld VHF with batteries packed separately
- Portable GPS
- 1 signal mirror
- Waterproof flashlight with batteries packed separately
- Spare flashlight batteries and bulbs
- Small plastic sextant with instructions
- Last year's Nautical Almanac
- Small scale chart of ocean in which you are sailing
- Protractor
- Pads of paper and 4 pencils
- Photocopy of passports
- Photocopy of ship's papers
- $100 cash

- Duplicate credit card
- Small container underwater epoxy
- Tube of silicone sealant and/or bedding compound
- Plastic bags
- Duct tape
- Pliers, screwdriver and adjustable wrench
- 1 wire saw
- 3 sizes Dacron sail thread, 200 feet of each
- 6 stainless steel sail needles
- At least 2 sharp knives, sheathed or folded
- Sharpening stone
- 100 feet each of 1/8-inch and 1/4-inch line
- 24 fishhooks, 1/2- to 1-inch, single and three-pronged
- Pork rind strips for bait
- 2 spools 80-lb. test fishing line
- 20 feet leader line
- 10 feet of 1/16-inch stainless steel seizing wire
- Rubber sandals or shoes (for rocky landfalls)
- 2 white towels
- 2 pair nylon stockings (for collecting plankton)
- Toothbrush and dental floss
- Space blanket (thermal blanket)
- Pair of sturdy gloves (hand protection)
- 2 long-sleeved shirts and two sweaters

- 2 sets polypropylene underwear

- 6 pocket-sized chemical heaters (from a camping store)

- Survival-at-sea manual

Post a list of additional gear to take from the ship if time allows, such as additional food, water and fishing gear, medical supplies, binoculars, charts, etc.

Man Overboard Rig

Another emergency situation for which all sailors have to prepare is a crewmember overboard. A proper man overboard rig includes a life buoy, such as a flotation horseshoe, with a drogue, within reach of the helmsman and ready for instant use. The life buoy should be equipped with a whistle, a dye marker, a self-igniting light, and a pole and flag attached to the life buoy with a 10-foot floating line. See ORC regulations 11.51 and 11.52 in Chapter 7. Add the man overboard rig to the list of things you must carry but hope to never use.

Rehearse the procedures and techniques for retrieving a crewmember from the water. It's not easy to lift a wet, unconscious adult back on board. Be sure you have a Lifesling or similar cradle that enables you to hoist a crewmember up onto the deck with a halyard. Practice the maneuver before you go. The life you save could be your own.

The M.O.M. (man overboard module) is a compact, self-inflating man overboard kit packed in a valise. This may or not be a case of taking a simple system and packaging it into a more complicated (and more expensive) one. In any case, the M.O.M. pack, the Lifesling and similar products are popular on modern yachts and you should be aware that they're available. The best way to become familiar with the most current safety products available is by perusing boat shows, boating magazines and chandleries.

Captain Tor's Last Chance Trip Line

Anyone who has ever sailed offshore shares a common dread: falling overboard and helplessly watching the boat sail away. No matter how many shipmates you have resting belowdecks, if you're alone on deck you're at risk just as much as the singlehanded sailor. No one will hear you cry out.

Most passagemakers take the obvious precautions: maintaining pulpits and stanchions with continuous lifelines around the yacht's rail; running jacklines along the side decks to clip on the safety harness that we wear *most* of the time. Some even tow a so-called safety line astern. Still, every so often we hear of the ultimate tragedy: Some sailor has fallen overboard and been lost at sea.

I've singlehanded quite a bit. Over time, I gave the problem some serious consideration. Now, I'd like to share an idea I came up with, tested and have used for years because, if properly installed by more sailors, it could save at least some of those lives. It's a simple, inexpensive lone-sailor-overboard rescue device that I call my Last Chance Trip Line.

If you were to grab onto a simple safety line trailing behind a boat sailing at five or six knots, you'd have a tough time trying to haul yourself forward on it while being dragged through the water. Fully clothed, it would be nearly impossible. Eventually, you'd tire out and let go. But the result of grabbing the Last Chance Trip Line is that the boat will almost immediately come to a near or complete halt, giving the man overboard an opportunity to easily regain the ship. It will work aboard any boat, providing one last chance to save yourself if the nightmare ever comes true and you find yourself overboard and alone while underway.

The Last Chance Trip Line consists of about 200 feet of 1/2" yellow polypropylene line (i.e., floating line), a Styrofoam ball float like the kind lobstermen commonly use to mark their traps, at least two 5-ft. pieces of 5/16" or 3/8" elastic shock cord with a plastic hook at one end, and one or two 1/2" blocks on lanyards. It'll also require a bit of trial-and-error experimentation because precisely how this equipment is assembled will vary from boat to boat. Here's the basic idea:

The buoyant trip line, which has half hitches tied in every 6 feet or so for better gripping, trails behind the boat while voyaging off-shore. The Styrofoam float marks the bitter end (pun intended), while the inboard end is led in such a way that increased drag on the trail-ing line will disengage the self-steering mechanism or engine throttle. In the case of a vessel under sail, it will then steer the boat up into the wind to stall it. Once you've worked out the right adjustments for your boat, you can set up your Last Chance Trip Line in a couple of minutes anytime you're heading out to sea.

The normal line tension on the line created by towing is coun-tered by the shock cord, hooked to a bight in the line two or three feet abaft the stern rail. Because of this, the inboard portion of the trip line remains slack until the weight of a dragging person overcomes the shock cord to exert force on the inboard line.

Now let's consider various ways in which this can be applied to ac-complish our goal of stopping the boat, beginning with disconnecting autopilots:

The external autopilot on a sailboat's tiller (Figure 15a) is the eas-iest to disengage—all it takes is a light lifting motion to jerk its drive arm off the tiller attachment knob. To do this, the inboard end of the trip line runs from the bight (a) to which the shock cord (b) is attached, over the pushpit rail (c) to give it some height, then through a block (d) lashed to the tiller immediately aft of the attachment point of the auto-pilot drive arm. The block hangs by its lanyard just a few inches below the tiller. Finally, the trip line runs across the cockpit and slightly forward to the lee rail where it is tied to a strong at-tachment point (e) which is only slightly higher than the tiller. This end is secured, taking

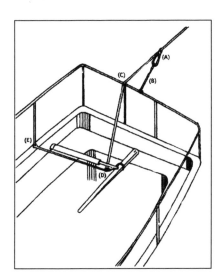

Figure 15a

up almost all of the slack in the trip line, but still allowing the shock cord to take the entire pulling force of the line trailing aft.

Because of the shock cord, the inboard end of the line remains slack (but just barely so), exerting no force on the autopilot or the tiller. But if someone in the water were to grab that trip line and drag behind the boat on it, the increased line tension would stretch the shock cord, putting tension directly on the trip line inboard of the bight. The taut trip line will raise the block, lifting the autopilot drive arm off the tiller, and it will simultaneously pull the tiller to leeward. The boat will head up, luff the sails, and stall. If the jib is trimmed for windward sailing, it will likely back, heaving the boat to. If the sails are trimmed for a reach, they'll likely continue luffing even it the boat falls off again. In any case, the man overboard has time to pull himself easily to the stalled boat.

Disengaging autopilots on boats with wheel steering requires variations of this principle, depending on the autopilot system used and how it is installed. (See Figure 15b) It may be necessary to run the trip line through a block on a short lanyard (a) tied to the autopilot's clutch knob so that it will, under tension, pull out the knob to disengage the self steering. The same principle applies to both wheel-hub clutches and to foot-level clutches found on some popular models. From the clutch block, the line passes through a second block (b) stationed to port or starboard of the helm, and then across to the wheel's rim (c) in order to have the ability to turn the boat. If the second block is on the lee side of the cockpit, the line's attachment point along the rim will be at the farthest (windward) spoke *below* the wheel's horizontal center plane. If the block is on the windward side, the line must be led to pull on the farthest (leeward) *high* spoke (as illustrated in Figure 15b) in

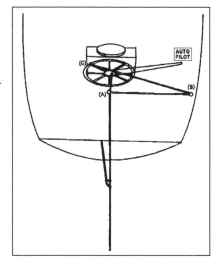

Figure 15b

order to turn the boat into the wind. Again, the shock cord aft holds the inboard line section barely slack until a strong pulling force is applied to the outboard end of the trip line.

On some boats a line-and-lanyard system might be easier to use (Figure 15c). Simply tie a second bight into the trip line, anywhere between the side block and the shock cord's bight. Lanyards, or short lengths of shock cord, can be easily led off a bight to pull clutch knobs and switches. Whatever directional pull it takes for a trip line to disengage the self-steering unit and/or head your boat into the wind can be engineered with blocks, shock cords, lanyards and a bit of ingenuity.

With internal autopilot units, a lanyard coming off the trip line may be led so that it flips a toggle switch that turns off the unit, allowing the trip line to turn the helm. Better still, a tug on the trip line could be rigged to activate an electric over-ride switch that will cause the autopilot to steer the boat sharply to windward. The same switch could also activate an alarm to arouse sleeping crew, but keeping it simple and self-reliant is probably best.

Windvanes pose no problem once you grasp the general idea of the Last Chance Trip Line. However, rather than disengaging the windvane, the trick here may be to use it to steer the boat into the

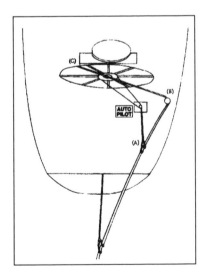

Figure 15c

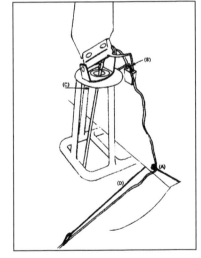

Figure 15d

wind. For example, on a Monitor windvane (Figure 15d), the trip line passes first through a block on a lanyard (a), then between the rods holding the vane's lead counterweight which is below the wind paddle (b), and finally ties to a convenient part of the windvane's framework (c) or ship's hardware. Once again, the shock cord (d) is attached to the trip line at the outboard bight, in this case just aft of the block. Because the shock cord keeps tension off the inboard section of the line, the windvane is free to operate unimpeded—until someone pulls on the trip line. Then the cocked windvane will steer the boat up into the wind, stalling her. By having the block on a lanyard, it's easy to shift its position and experiment to determine the correct angle of pull on the windvane's counterweight. This changes as the windvane paddle is swiveled for different points of sail. In this manner, you control which way the windvane will turn the boat when the trip line is pulled.

Lastly, stopping a boat that is motoring is as simple as rigging the line or lanyard to pull back the throttle, or the throttle and gearshift levers, or the engine cut-off knob. After reviewing the above variations of leading and balancing the trip line, an engine-stopper should be easy to figure out aboard your own boat.

As a boat's sailing speed increases, it may be necessary to tighten the shock cord. Otherwise, the increased drag on the line could overcome the shock cord and trip the system. The tension of the shock cord is adjusted from the inboard end so that the cord continues to barely overcome the pulling force of the dragging trip line, but beware of using too short a shock cord. It may not have enough stretch left in it to allow the trip line to work when needed. When adjusting for increased boat speed, it's generally better to re-tie the shock cord further forward on the boat rather than to shorten it. If this still isn't enough to overcome the drag or if the shock cord is stretched nearly to its limit, double up on the shock cord with a second piece. Ultimately, the shock cord must absorb the towing force with elasticity to spare.

Your Last Chance Trip Line system is easy to test without throwing your mate overboard. Just reach over the stern rail, beyond the shock cord, and haul firmly and steadily on the line. A safer alternative is to tie a bite in the line just abaft the shock cord attachment point, slide the end of a boat hook into it, and push to create the drag effect. If the boat comes to a halt, you got it right.

Once the trip line has done its job and allowed the lone sailor to pull himself back to the boat, he still must be able to climb aboard unassisted. A permanent ladder or steps installed at the transom, or some means for a swimmer to pull down a stern boarding ladder, will ensure a happy ending to the man overboard self-rescue.

By the way, the polypropylene trip line should be stored out of the sun when not in use. Otherwise, it will deteriorate rapidly from exposure to UV-rays.

You might argue that at night the trip line could be difficult to find quickly enough for a frightened person grappling in the dark. Or that it's useless to an unconscious man overboard. And that nothing takes the place of exercising proper caution to ensure that crewmembers don't fall off the boat in the first place. You'd be right. The Last Chance Trip Line is no substitute for wearing your safety harness while on deck, nor is it a 100% guaranteed lifesaver in every situation. But for the lone mariner who suddenly finds himself overboard while the boat sails on without him, the Last Chance Trip Line is a whole lot better than the alternative—no chance at all.

Emergency Hull Repair Kit

A cruising sailor has to be prepared to patch his hull if it becomes punctured or cracked. If a vessel is holed in a place made inaccessible by interior liner or paneling, a hatchet and crow bar may be needed to get to the problem area quickly from the inside, so carry some wrecking tools aboard. I also believe in carrying scraps of wood—short lengths of 2 x 4, storable pieces of 1/4" and 1/2" plywood—that may aid in temporarily blocking up a hole in the hull. Pieces of linoleum may work well for this. Linoleum is flexible and readily accepts epoxy. Also useful are self-tapping screws to fasten these patches to fiberglass.

A typical first line of defense with a large puncture could include stuffing a seat cushion into the hole, then bracing it in place with the scrap wood. With the water flow thus slowed to an amount more manageable by the bilge pumps, further repair can be made to get the vessel to port. Carry a bag of fiberglass cloth and mat, and several tubes of underwater epoxy for effecting temporary, in-water repairs. Pretreated cloth, ready to cure underwater, is available to buy. Keep a can of fiberglass resin, some fiberglass mat and cloth and a grinder aboard for making permanent repairs when you're finally able to dry the boat out by hauling or careening.

A plastic, waterproof tarpaulin or army-type ground cloth can be slung underneath the boat in an emergency to slow or stop water flooding in by being sucked up against the hole. The tarp is submerged at the bow, and crewmen on either side deck work lines from each of its corners aft. A sail can also be used for this emergency, stopgap measure. Another method, called "fothering" or "foddering", is the treatment for wooden boats with leaking seams and involves packing oakum into a sail, which is then manipulated beneath the hull. On a wooden yacht with, say, a leaking garboard, a diver may more accurately place a can-full of sawdust. Uncovering the can just beneath the leaking seam lets the sawdust float up and be sucked into the crack, where it expands and clogs the space.

Chapter 9

~~

The Boat Interior

Behold the macho sailor. Not only is he a terror on deck, but he's often a masochist below. He eats gruel out of the pot, bathes only in cold seawater, and packs an old sleeping bag for bedding!

Remember, friends, a cruising sailboat is a home. It's the year-around dwelling for us and, if we're lucky, our devoted mates. While there are inevitable compromises made, we don't have to emulate a military outpost, or duplicate the frugality of the pioneers. Whatever comforts and idiosyncratic pleasures we permit ourselves aboard, we certainly deserve.

Even before comfort are safety considerations. For example, non-skid on the companionway ladder is a must. Solid handrails and grabrails should be strategically placed throughout a boat's interior so that you can move from handhold to handhold, the length and breadth of the cabins, when the boat is in motion. Round off, pad, and other-wise eliminate all sharp corners belowdecks. We'll cover more interior safety precautions shortly.

Bunks

Most sailboat interiors of old were designed for a few celibate men to rough it for a brief trip, then go home. Today many of us live aboard full time and cruise as couples, which can be much more fun. We prefer a double bed for sleeping in port, and reserve the single berths for offshore. My previous boat featured a double diagonal berth in the fore-castle. It was the most comfortable berth when not underway, with a large opening hatch overhead for ventilation. When underway, the captain slept in the quarter berth, close to the companionway and the nav station. The crew used the port and starboard settees, which are usually more comfortable. In really rough weather, the best bunk on most boats is a mattress on the cabin sole, closest to the center of gravity.

If your boat has a separate aft cabin it may have or be able to ac-commodate a centerline island queen bed, which in my opinion is ideal for a cruising couple. It allows both of you to get in and out of bed easily, without one having to climb over the other as is the case with a double bunk set diagonally or athwartships. One or both of you will want to be able to use this bed offshore, too. The aft cabin expe-riences less motion than cabins forward when beating to windward. However, when you're beating and the boat's heeled over, you'll need bunk boards or lee cloths running lengthwise to hold sleepers secure. One bunk board should be made to fit along either the port or star-board side of the bed. If you split the mattress and bottom sheets lengthwise, you can make provisions for a removable centerline bunk board, as well, so that two people can sleep in the bed without piling on top of one another.

The most impractical yet most common double bunk on sailboats, the V-berth, requires the acrobatic maneuver of swinging your body around 180° to get in and out. This can get tiresome after a while. The long-term sleeping arrangement on your boat depends on her layout and your willingness or ability to make changes. Since we spend one third of our lives in bed, it's worth giving some thought and effort to making it comfortable.

How well we sleep aboard, particularly offshore, is important. A rested crew is a happier group, and a rested captain makes fewer mis-takes. All berths need to have adequate ventilation, including a 12-volt fan, and a directional reading light to permit some to read while oth-ers sleep. The optimum single bunk for most of us is at least 6'6" long and 24 to 30 inches wide. The mattress is 3 or 4 inches of foam rub-ber. There's a removable, padded bunk board or a lee cloth to retain the occupant in rough conditions. Bedding includes sheets, a real pillow, and blankets—just like home. Form-fitted bottom sheets, purchased or home sewn, are best because they are easy to put on and they stay in place. Sleeping bags are reserved for cold weather cruising or sleeping out in the cockpit. Above all, of course, bunks need to be kept dry.

Cushions

Whether you're buying a new boat or refurbishing a used one, order several yards of spare, matching interior cushion fabric and stow it away somewhere. The time will come when you need to re-cover just one or two cushions that have been stained, burned, torn, worn or otherwise damaged beyond repair. Any but the most basic fabrics will long since have gone out of production and will be unavailable. Use comfortable, breathable fabrics, not vinyl. Concerning fabric color, dark fabrics make the interior feel smaller, more confining. Lighter colors have the opposite effect. Pastels like beige, with or without patterns, won't show the dirt as readily as white.

You can treat clean interior cushion fabric with Scotchguard, available in aerosol spray cans. Scotchguard makes fabrics somewhat water-resistant and easier to wipe clean, and protects them from absorbing dirt, body oil and stains. Buy a case of the stuff, haul all your cushions out onto a quiet dock on a clear day, and spray them all over with at least two coats, allowing each coat time to dry as per the directions.

The backs of all vertical cushions can be made to have envelope-like pockets for chart storage. Round and square pillow covers can be stuffed with off-season clothing and extra bedding as a handy way to store these items.

Colors

A light interior is easier to live in, especially when it's raining for the fourth day in a row and you're cooped up belowdecks. If your saloon is over-laden with dark teak or mahogany, consider refinishing some of the broad bulkhead surfaces with light-colored, easy-to-clean Formica or tile. The same effect is accomplished by applying a couple of coats of cream white paint (after first sealing the wood with varnish), especially on the overhead and the dark corners back against the hull and under the side decks. Set off by natural wood trim, this can be very attractive and you'll be amazed at how much brighter and larger your boat will feel.

Bringing in more daylight through larger portholes, Lexan hatches, and deck prisms will also help lighten and enlarge a gloomy interior. So will a mounted mirror on the main saloon bulkhead.

Electric Lighting

Years ago, I lived and cruised aboard a very basic, some might say austere 1927 gaff-rigged ketch. The youngest item aboard AUTANT was her captain. The boat possessed no engine and no instruments other than a beautifully binnacled compass. The only ship's batteries were the D-cells in the flashlight. What all this has to do with electric lights aboard the modern cruising sailboat is beyond me, except that having lived without for nearly 3 years, I don't think I'll ever take them for granted.

The three common categories of interior DC lights in today's yachts are:

- Ordinary incandescent overhead lamps, several in the main saloon and at least one per cabin or compartment. Some offer the alternative of switching on a red (night) light, which permits visibility below without destroying your night vision. High/low intensity switches (or dimmer switches) on lights save power and enhance ambiance for different occasions.

- Directional reading lights, one per berth and one, with a moveable red filter or polarized dimmer lens, in the nav station. These bright bulbs use up the most electricity.

- Fluorescent lights make a cold but energy efficient light, using less power than the others do. If you need to keep a light burning all night, for example to acclimate new crew underway, this is a good light to use. SPARROW had two in the galley area and one recessed in a saloon bookshelf. Non-isolated fluorescent lights may interfere with electronics performance such as GPS reception, so be sure yours are isolated.

You'll want to have good lighting in the engine compartment. Also, you might carry one or two small AC table lamps for cabin illumination dockside, to conserve the ship's batteries and 12-volt bulbs when shore power is available.

Oil Lamps

Traditional, decorative kerosene or paraffin lamps are consistent with the philosophy of having a simple back up for every system on the boat. If/when the electric lights fail, a couple of gimbaled kerosene lamps will help you make it through the night. Even when the 12-volt lighting is functioning, the glow of an oil lamp makes the cabin cozier, and adds some real warmth to a chilly evening. A mirror or a plate of polished stainless steel mounted behind the lamp will nearly double the brilliance. Use cleaner burning mineral spirits in lieu of kerosene for fuel. Carry a hurricane lamp to display on deck as an alternative anchor light. This also serves as pleasant cockpit lighting for evenings under the stars.

Entertainment

Treat yourself and your boat to a decent CD and cassette tape player and AM/FM radio. I often like to record the local music from radio stations as I travel. Unfortunately, most of the so-called marine cassette players do not record. So I bought a dual cassette AM/FM portable stereo recorder/player, a "boom box." I adapted it to 12-volt using an inexpensive Radio Shack 12V-9V converter, and mounted it in the saloon. Auxiliary speakers in the cockpit can liven up the watch. Headphones that reach or plug in at the cockpit allow the night watch to enjoy music without disturbing sleeping crew. Ahhh, a starry night, a fair breeze and Mozart!

This is also a good time to think about bringing along that musical instrument you used to play a little, or always wished you could. It's never too late to learn.

Speaking of playing, stash a few games aboard if you're so inclined. Chess, checkers, Scrabble, Monopoly, and a deck of cards can provide hours of entertainment for crew and guests. Computer games are a modern alternative.

One of the great delights of the cruising life is that it allows time for reading. Bring along plenty of paperbacks that, once read, can be swapped with other sailors. Book swapping is a popular way to meet your neighbors in harbor.

In some areas, particularly in many West Indies yacht harbors, movie swapping has become a regular practice among cruisers. More and more boats have TVs, VCRs and DVD players aboard with a stash of movies. People tend to hang on to their movie library, swapping films for the evening and retrieving them in the morning. If you don't have a DC/AC power inverter aboard, you'll need a 12-volt television and video player. Ideally, purchase a TV that has switchable reception capability. Ordinary models don't work in many other countries because broadcasting frequencies vary internationally. An external antenna will greatly enhance television reception.

Of course, lots of cruisers don't have VCRs aboard their boats. I occasionally invited half a dozen sailors over to SPARROW for a movie night. I set up the VCR/TV on the companionway hatch and we all sat out under the stars in the cockpit, enjoying a good flick and munching popcorn. Cruising ain't what it used to be, but it sure is fun.

Oh, by the way, you might want to have a string of Christmas lights or other special decorations aboard to dress the ship for the holidays.

Fans

Install 12-volt electric fans aboard, at least one for each cabin. As mentioned above, make sure every berth can be cooled by a fan. The nav station and especially the galley should also have a fan available, even if they share one. There are some pricey electric boat fans available in chandleries, but small 12-volt fans are much less expensive if purchased from an auto parts store. They work as well as the fancy ones, sometimes better.

Screens

For the world-cruising sailor, mosquito screens are an absolute necessity. Every porthole, hatch, and companionway need to be opened in hot weather, but screened to keep out the little vampires. Soft hatch screens, snap-on and/or framed in Velcro, are often easier to stow than screens mounted on rigid frames. For luxurious living aboard in the tropics, you can screen in your entire cockpit. Ask your local canvas shop for ideas on how to do that on your particular boat.

Aboard SPARROW I had a big screen tent, purchased for $4 from an army surplus store, which draped over the boom gallows and covered the companionway. This enabled me to stand in the companionway and look out without going outside. The mesh was even fine enough to stop those flying teeth called no-see-ums. These insects, disguised as gnats, are really tiny demons from hell sent to torture mankind beyond reasonable endurance. No-see-ums are repelled by Avon Skin-So-Soft and Off insect repellent, but do not seem deterred by Cutter brand repellent. I've discovered that they tend to leave if I burn incense aboard, which also makes the boat smell nice.

Cabin Heater

If your cruising plans include non-tropical regions, a cabin heater may be invaluable. I chose a propane cabin heater for the same reason I prefer propane for cooking; it's a clean and available fuel. My Force 10 brand heater did a fine job of keeping SPARROW's cabin warm through a couple of chilly Mediterranean winters, though it needed a low powered electric fan installed on the bulkhead to blow across its top in order to move the heated air around the cabin a bit. Also, the heater's exhaust pipe cap on deck, the "Charlie Noble," had to be covered during heavy weather to keep water from entering.

Flame-driven cabin heaters burn oxygen so you absolutely must allow enough fresh air in to keep from suffocating yourself. The Force 10 included a very sensitive oxygen depletion sensor that would automatically shut the unit off if it wasn't getting enough fresh air, a valuable safety precaution. Suffocation in boat cabins, caused by heaters burning up all the oxygen, claims lives every year. Be sure to leave at least one porthole open whenever you're using any flame-driven appliance.

Because a cabin heater may be on many hours a day, it can burn up a lot of propane, which becomes expensive and, in some places, inconvenient to replenish. An alternative is a properly designed and installed diesel-fueled heater. Diesel is relatively cheap. There are many in-cabin diesel heaters on the market, but high-latitude cruising friends tell me the Espar *forced air* diesel heater is the way to go if you can afford it, although its heating ducts take up valuable storage space as they snake through the boat's bilges and lockers. One excellent feature of forced-air heaters like the Espar is that the combustion takes place outside of the cabin, since the unit is mounted in some separate compartment in the boat and the hot air is then forced through ducts into the living quarters by an electric fan. When shore power is available, you can use a small electric ceramic cube heater to conserve fuel.

Many heated boats suffer from hull condensation. This is a serious problem, causing mildew that can ruin clothes and other stored gear, and stain interior liners. Cored hulls and decks help alleviate this problem. Non-cored boats can benefit by the installation of insulation, such as neoprene panels, or even carpeting, glued against the hull. Metal-framed hatches and portholes will often sweat and may occasionally need some kind of water drip catcher beneath them, if only a towel or rag.

Air Conditioning

The decision of whether or not to install air conditioning in your boat is, like most equipment decisions, a matter of personal priorities and budget. In my experience, air conditioning is a wonderful luxury, but not really necessary for cruisers who live primarily at anchor, even in the tropics. A complete set of deck awnings combined with good hatch ventilation, screens, and a few 12-volt fans will usually keep temperatures comfortable, or at least bearable, in the hottest climates if there is any kind of a breeze passing through the boat.

Of course, if you tend to stay at docks a lot in hot, humid areas, an air conditioner that can at least run off shore power might be very worthwhile. I lived aboard in a Miami marina for a while and used a simple, inexpensive RV unit that sat over the main saloon hatch. It made life aboard very comfortable indeed, especially during the brutal summer months, and when I eventually took off cruising I simply gave it away to a friend. Similarly, you can just stick a small, ordinary household window air conditioner in the companionway when you're at the dock, stepping over it to enter and exit.

A light-weight, relatively inexpensive alternative that might be a reasonable compromise for many boaters is the Krusin Kool portable air conditioner made by Aqua Cal. Built into a hard shell suitcase, this modern marvel is easy to use, easy to move and easy to stow away, although it can be permanently installed. At 7,000 BTUs, it's adequate for most 27-30' boats. Two units would cool down a bigger vessel nicely, or you can use one unit to cool just the cabin you're in—the saloon during the daytime and your sleeping quarters at night. The Krusin Kool weighs 56 lbs., measures 26"L x 21.5"H x 9"W, consumes just 5.5 amps at 115 VAC total, and only costs about $1,000. Of course, you'll still need a source of AC electricity to power it, if only a hefty power inverter. The inverter must be capable of handling a surge of 20 amps @ 120 VAC, 60Hz and have a continuous surge rating of that capacity to handle the starting load when the unit cycles.

A proper, installed marine air conditioning system, such as a typical 16,000-BTU single split unit with reverse cycle heat, will cost between $5,000 and $8,000, and you'll need a generator to run it away from the dock. Such a unit is usually a direct-expansion seawater-cooled air conditioning system that cools by removing heat and moisture from the cabin. The heat is absorbed by the refrigerant, which flows through sealed tubes and is then transferred into the seawater, which is pumped through the system and discharged overboard. When the refrigerant flow is reversed, the opposite is true. Heat is extracted from the seawater, electrically amplified, and used to warm the air flowing into the living area.

Air conditioning size requirements are directly proportional to the volume of space you want to cool. To determine how big a system you'll need, the general rule of thumb is 14 BTUs per cubic foot of air-conditioned space. Figure a bit higher for extreme conditions, and a bit less for just cooling staterooms in the evening. You can hire a professional to prepare a thermodynamic heat load analysis for your particular vessel. In individual staterooms you may wish to have small, separate systems that are independently controlled, and one large system for the main saloon and galley areas.

Ventilation and Deodorizing

Give some attention to the flow of air through your boat's interior, especially if you plan to cruise in tropical climates. Lots of hatches and ports that open are a big plus. If your boat doesn't have a big, opening hatch over the main saloon, consider installing one. Also, an opening port in the quarter berth (facing the cockpit) brings light and air into an otherwise stuffy space. Solar powered exhaust fans mounted on hatches help move air through if the boat is to be left closed for any length of time.

Traditional dorade vents work well, bringing in air when faced into the wind and drawing it out when faced away from the wind. They ventilate the interior offshore when the boat is otherwise closed up, most effectively if positioned over sea berths. Dorade boxes prevent water from entering the boat in moderate conditions, but the cutout must be designed to be plugged (with a screw-in cap) in very heavy weather. It also needs to be screened in buggy harbors.

Windscoops, panels usually made of light nylon that are hung over open hatches, guide breezes into the boat in port. At anchor, with the boat lying head to the wind, the simplest designs do the job. Dockside, the more costly four-directional models are best since they don't need to be reset for each wind shift.

The ship's head is often the space least ventilated, yet the most badly in need of it. In SPARROW's head, I had the builder install a small opening hatch that I habitually left open in fair weather. It not only kept the head compartment fresher, but also made showering more pleasant under warm skies. The head's porthole was always left open, except when beating to windward on a starboard tack. If a little rainwater occasionally came in, it did no harm.

Keeping that little water closet from becoming smelly is important. It affects your whole living environment. The toilet has to be flushed very thoroughly every time it's used—not just until the bowl looks clear, but until the hoses are completely purged (a minimum of 20 pump strokes was standard procedure on SPARROW). Otherwise, it becomes the source of an unpleasant odor that can permeate a small vessel in spite of ventilation. Here's a little trick to help keep the toilet clean, clear and fresh: Occasionally pour a cup of white vinegar into the bowl with just a cup or so of water in it. Then pump the toilet handle a couple of strokes and leave the solution in there overnight. The vinegar dissolves built up deposits in the working parts and hoses, and it eliminates unpleasant odors. Your toilet will live longer and smell sweeter.

Sink and shower drains need to be cleaned regularly, too. Shower drainage directly into the bilges is unsanitary and unacceptable. This gray water should ideally pump directly overboard from a shower water collection pan under a grate in the shower compartment. Second best (because it requires more regular cleaning) is a separate sump container in the bilge with overboard pump-out. An electric sump pump activated by a float switch, with a screened or filtered intake hose, works best to empty a bilge shower sump.

Holding tanks obviously have to be absolutely airtight, aside from the outboard air vent. Regular pumping, occasional cleaning and chemical deodorizing, especially before an offshore passage, will minimize the potential for odors emanating from this modern-day yachting requirement. At sea, most cruisers re-direct the toilet discharge overboard by means of a Y-valve in the hose line, reserving the holding tank for use in port.

Another source of odor aboard is the galley. Food smells great while it's cooking, but not so great if the odor lingers halfway through the next day. A large opening port above the stove is a good idea. If the galley is not located adjacent to the companionway hatch, an overhead hatch or an exhaust fan may be needed to help eliminate smoke and steam. In any case, the cook will appreciate good ventilation, which should include a 12-volt fan nearby. An open box of baking soda absorbs odors in a refrigerator or ice chest. Keep sink and ice box drains clean. Food particles smell as they decay.

The ship's chain locker stays damp if it's not ventilated. Mud and bits of seaweed collect and ferment and can emit a dank odor into the forepeak. A dorade or a solar vent installed on the foredeck above the locker helps solve this problem in port, although they must be removed and capped offshore. At least, leave the anchor deck pipes open in port to air things out. Occasionally rinsing the anchor chain and rode helps, as does a periodic chain locker scrub down and drying. I do both just prior to each offshore passage.

The engine and the bilges are also olfactory offenders. Neither needs to smell of oil sludge and diesel fuel, though they do in an awful lot of boats. It's a simple matter to keep them clean. If you're consistent about it, is not a big deal. There should be a drip pan, gel-coated or painted white and separate from the bilge, underneath the engine to catch oil. An absorbent pad in the pan will help keep oil out of the bilge. Clean both the engine and drip pan with de-greaser and paper towels, at least with every oil change. Scrub the bilges with soap and water and bleach until they are spotless. Then finish the job by pouring in a cup or so of Ecover brand detergent. This is the only environmentally safe detergent I know of that lathers reasonably well in salt water. In the bilge, it will clean and emulsify small amounts of oil as it sloshes around with any water that finds its way in.

Ventilating storage spaces forestalls mildew. Louvered, caned or decoratively cut-out locker doors and sides will help, as will periodic cleaning out of all compartments. Items stored in hammocks get plenty of fresh air.

Good ventilation combined with good cleaning habits will keep your floating home a fresh and pleasant place to live.

Storage

It seems to be an axiom that no matter how large or small the vessel, it will be filled to overflowing by the time we go cruising. Storage is largely a function of the boat's size and design. Usually, the best we can do is to minimize the extraneous odds and ends we bring aboard, and maximize use of existing spaces.

By compartmentalizing lockers and even bilges, and by opening access to cubbyholes left inaccessible by the builder, we can fit an incredible amount of gear into our compact quarters. Adding shelves for books, tools, cans, etc. will turn flat bulkheads and tall lockers into efficient storage space. Converting an unnecessary bunk, like a pilot berth or part of an oversized quarter berth, turns rarely used space into large permanent bins for provisions. Small hammocks are great space makers, strung up in corners under the decks to hold clothing or bedding, or in the galley to hold produce (see Figure 16). In many

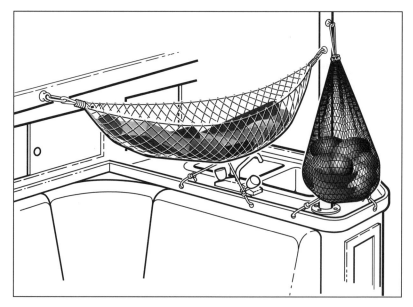

Figure 16: Hammocks and net bags increase a boat's storage capacity by utilizing otherwise wasted space. They let their contents get plenty of fresh air, too—perfect for anything from vegetables to clothing.

sailboats, the cockpit coaming is a dry, hollow space that can be accessed from inside the cockpit lockers or from belowdecks to stow rolled charts, clothing, toilet paper, or food in hammocks. Magazine racks fit up against flat, narrow spaces like the inside of the hull under the nav table. Mounting hooks or snaps on bulkheads lets you hang canvas bags for more storage. Larger vessels may have space on deck for one or more deck boxes. Using space efficiently and thoroughly is the name of the game.

It's easy and inexpensive to line the clothing hanging lockers with cedar. This creates a pleasant scent and repels moths and fleas. Speaking of hanging lockers, do not use metal clothes hangers. Use plastic only or you'll eventually have a locker full of rust-stained clothing. Phosphoric acid, bottled under brand names such as Ospho and Chemprime, will make rust stains disappear in minutes without damaging most fabrics. It is often sold in marine and hardware stores, and has a number of uses aboard.

One trick that helps alleviate the storage crunch is to box up extra clothes and other things that you "just might need." Label the boxes with their contents and leave them ashore in storage, or with a friend or relative. Then, after you've been cruising for a while, you can send for what you need, or exchange one set of clothes for another to have the variety without the overload. Or you may forget all about that stuff, which means you never really needed it aboard anyhow.

Wardrobe planning for liveaboard cruising is, naturally, a personal thing. Most neophytes bring far too many clothes. In many foreign countries, commercial washing machines are non-existent, let alone dry cleaning facilities. So leave the fancy fabrics and expensive dress clothes behind. Most clothes should fold, not hang. For cool climates, layered clothing is preferable to thick clothing. Of course, you may well want to dress up once in a while for a night on the town, so pack one or two outfits for these occasions. But the rule of thumb is, less is better.

When stowing gear aboard, try to keep heavy items—tools and the like—as near to the boat's center of gravity as possible. That is, place this heavy equipment in low-lying lockers amidship. Avoid weighing down the lazarette and forepeak, as this will increase the boat's tendency to hobbyhorse in a seaway. This is especially true of hulls designed with long overhangs.

Wet Locker

Think about where you'll stow your rain gear aboard. Many mid-size sailboats have a cramped little space designated as the *wet locker*, but if you were to put wet rain jackets in there they'd come out green with mildew the next time you need them. Rain gear should be stowed away dry, so it may as well be in a hammock or a cupboard as in an undersized wet locker. When foul-weather gear has been used, hang it on hooks in the head or shower compartment. There it can drip water harmlessly, and can air out. When the weather settles and the gear has dried, it stows away either hung up or folded on a shelf. Of course, larger boats can afford the luxury of a proper, ventilated wet locker.

Securing For Capsize

If the Jolly Green Giant picked up your boat, turned it upside down, and shook it—maybe even dropped it—what would happen to the equipment aboard? This is a serious question to consider, because Mother Ocean can turn into a very nasty green giant and do exactly that. A sturdy vessel may well survive being capsized or rolled over intact, but the crew below decks may be in grave danger of injury from flying objects. It's seaman-like to stow things carefully; even a rough windward beat will dislodge much of what you thought was secure. A capsize will empty nearly every locker on the boat if you haven't latched them properly. Tools, pots and cans may all suddenly become lethal projectiles.

Visualize your boat first sideways, then upside down. Now go through her foot by foot and list every single thing that's going to come adrift. Running through this little exercise now may save you much grief later.

For example, the offshore cruising sailboat ought to have all floorboards held firmly in place. I had the builder do this on SPARROW using stout bronze fittings distributed by ABI. Your local marine chandlery can order them for you and any carpenter handy with a router and a drill can install them. They recess into the floorboards, flush with the cabin sole, and only open if you lift the handle and turn it (see Figure 17). Simple, strong latches of wood or metal that pivot on a center bolt can secure locker lids. Remember to latch the icebox and chart table tops. Stretch a shock cord or two over the shelved books while offshore. The galley stove may be designed to lift out of its gimbal, but should have a strong safety latch to prevent this happening accidentally during a capsize. Ship's batteries have to be strapped, bilge pumps screwed down and anchors lashed while offshore. Secure everything aboard to stay put if the boat capsizes.

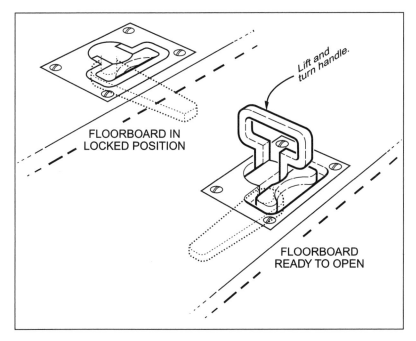

Figure 17: Floorboards need special fittings to be securely latched in case of a capsize.

Thwarting Thieves

To a thief, every yachtsman is wealthy and a boat is easy pickings. To the cruising sailor, there are few things more upsetting than coming aboard to find your home ransacked, valuable possessions stolen, your sanctuary violated. Keelhaul the bastards, I say!

It is worthwhile to take some preventive measures to deter crooks. Most petty thieves rely on darkness and solitude to conceal their dirty deeds. Most are also lazy by nature (if they were willing to work hard for their livelihood, they wouldn't be stealing). So make it light, noisy, and difficult for them and they're more likely to leave your boat alone.

Aboard SPARROW I concocted a simple and effective combination of deterrents. Part one was keeping them out. This included replacing the screwed teak companionway trim boards with heavy bronze (or stainless) flat bar, cut to shape and through bolted with carriage bolts. This made it nearly impossible to break in with a crow bar. The lock was a recessed type that could not be cut with a hacksaw or bolt cutter. Also, there was a simple bolt lock inside to lock out intruders while we sleep.

Still, a determined thief can bash his way into a fiberglass or wood boat no matter what you do. So, phase two included a very loud alarm bell wired to disconnect switches at the hatches, which also triggered bright deck lights. The clincher was a pair of mace or tear gas canisters mounted at the companionway with trip cords triggered by opening the hatch. One can was angled to empty into the face of the intruder; the other was directed into the saloon, thus rendering the cabin uninhabitable for a while. A bit excessive, you say? You won't think so once you've been robbed.

Dinghy theft is the most common theft problem cruisers face. Lock the outboard motor to the dinghy. Chain the dinghy to piers and docks when you're ashore. At night, lock it to your boat. Better still, use a halyard to hoist your dinghy aboard or alongside amidship, or raise it into the davits if you have them. Lock oars to the dink's seat and store other items in a locked locker. An inflatable tender with a 15- to 25-horsepower outboard motor is the most popular target for dinghy thieves. Rowboats and small outboards are less likely to be stolen, but certainly aren't immune. Some sailors paint their dinghies, including inflatables, with wild or distinctive colors to make them less attractive to a thief because they'd be harder to resell. The last time I bought a brand new outboard motor, I painted the cover a flat white to make the motor look older. It's unfortunate, but that's the way it is in some ports.

For the dinghy, I like the bronze or stainless steel Sesame locks, which allow you to decide the 4-digit combination. Invest in padlocks for all deck lockers on the ship. Single key series locks are worth the extra price. All locks that go to sea should be made entirely of bronze, brass and stainless steel. Still, they need periodic lubrication with white lithium grease.

Lock up the liferaft in port. When away from the boat for any length of time, disconnect the main engine's starter, or at the very least leave the fuel shut-off stopper engaged. Look at your boat from the point of view of the thief, and then do everything you can to make it difficult for him.

Guns

If you carry guns aboard, keep copies of a list showing the makes, serial numbers, and exact amount of ammunition you have for each weapon. You'll often need to present this information when you clear into a foreign country. Some foreign authorities will take the weapons off the boat, to be returned when you leave. Sometimes rifles are more acceptable to officials than pistols. Automatic and military type weapons are usually not welcomed in host countries. Favorite rifles among cruisers include the sawed off riot shotgun (minimum legal barrel length in the U.S. is 18"), and the stainless steel Mini-14 high-powered semi-automatic made by Sturm, Ruger and Co.

Some countries will allow guns to remain aboard if they're in a locked cabinet. A discreet, lockable gun locker is a good idea.

Alternative weapons that generally won't attract the attention of authorities include: club, cutlass (knives, machete, etc.), crossbow, and a black belt in Kung Fu. Depending on where you cruise, pepper spray, spear guns and flare guns are sometimes, but not always, considered weapons and you may be required to declare them. There is, I am told, a device that converts a 25-mm flare gun into a one-shot pistol capable of firing a shotgun cartridge.

Chapter 10

The Galley

I'm the first to admit I'm not much of a cook. (The next to admit it is anyone who's ever eaten my cooking.) But I sure do appreciate good cooking, and I do everything I can to let my mate know it.

Unfortunately, in many small sailboats the galley gets the short end of the designer's stick, as if it were an afterthought. A tiny stove is shoved to one side of the companionway ladder and crewmembers have to squeeze past the poor cook en route to and from the cockpit. Surely both the source and the creator of our meals afloat deserve more consideration.

Stoves and Stove Fuel

Ideally, your ship's stove will include an oven with a broiler, as well as two or more top burners. It will be of stainless steel construction and gimbaled to remain level while the boat rolls. Moveable clamp retainers on the stovetop will keep pots and pans in place. A stout horizontal bar between the cook and the stove is a necessary safety feature to prevent someone from being thrown into the stove underway. A belt-like strap is also a good idea, to keep the cook from being thrown out of the galley. The stove should be provided with a simple barrel bolt to lock it in place, to prevent excessive swinging when not in use in rough weather. Remember, too, that the unit must be secure in the event of capsize.

How the stove's burners are fueled is important. Denatured alcohol (stove alcohol) is certainly the worst choice. It is terribly expensive, burns with a comparatively cool flame, is virtually unavailable in most foreign ports, and its fumes are the only thing I know that can make me seasick. The one point in its favor is that its flame is extinguishable with water.

The next least desirable stove fuel is diesel. Diesel-fueled burners have a tendency to clog and require frequent disassembly and cleaning. On the plus side, the fuel is inexpensive and readily available in most ports of call.

Kerosene is the old purist's choice of stove fuel and provides a good, hot flame. I used it for many years on several of my boats (although I substituted mineral spirits, which burns cleaner). However, even if you get used to the preheating process, which requires a squirt of alcohol, the cleaning and repairing of the burners is almost as constant a chore as with diesel burners. So is cleaning up the soot from the flame when you fail to pre-heat the burner sufficiently. Also, kerosene has become all but impossible to find in many foreign ports.

That brings us to the modern sailors' choice, liquid propane gas (LPG). You can usually use butane gas in propane systems, which is a good thing since some ports only have butane available. Properly installed and regularly checked, a propane system is safe. It is also clean, efficient, and inexpensive to use. Best of all, it's available in or near most major ports today. SPARROW used propane for cabin and water heating, as well as for cooking. She carried two 20-lb. tanks. Depending on climate, we got one to three months use per tank, and a refill costs only about $10 on the U.S. East Coast today. That's not a bad utility bill.

However, don't ever forget that propane and butane gases are heavier than air and will flow down to the bilges if they leak inside the boat. If enough gas accumulates and a spark ignites it, it explodes. You could loose more than your boat. So you really have to be conscientious about installing, using and inspecting the system.

Gas bottles should be in a deck box or in an airtight locker ventilated so that any leaks will run directly overboard. Install a propane sniffer (a gas detector with alarm) in the bilge. Use electric solenoid switches for each appliance to shut off gas at the source with a switch in the galley. Install a single, continuous gas line between the solenoid and the appliance. Check the whole system regularly and often by dabbing a solution of liquid soap and water on each connection. It'll bubble if there's a leak. Also test by shutting off the tank valve while the solenoid switches are open, then watching the pressure gauge for any rapid pressure decline indicating a leak in the system. When you're finished cooking, it's good practice to shut off the solenoid switch before shutting off the stove control, letting the flame burn up all the gas remaining in the line. This way, there is no gas left in the line that could possibly leak into the bilges. In many (but not all) countries including the U.S., an odor is added to propane to facilitate detection.

There is one other alternative to LPG. That is CNG (compressed natural gas). CNG is lighter than air and is supposed to rise up out of the boat if it leaks. However, it can gather up under decks and hollow coamings, so it can be just as dangerous, just as potentially explosive as leaking LPG. Anyway, it's not available in most ports like LPG is, so it's not practical for the global or even the coastal voyager.

In the United States, propane tanks must be inspected and stamped every five years. Some countries have more stringent laws governing the installation, use and refilling of gas bottles. Many foreign countries use bottle fittings different from the standard U.S. fitting. To refill your tanks, you may have to fabricate adapters for different regions, using a length of hose with a male fitting that'll screw into your tank at one end, and the locally-used tank-head fitting that accepts their pump nozzle at the other. So, pack a spare male fitting, hose and hose clamps.

It's a good idea to have a back-up cooking system aboard. I kept a small, single burner kerosene stove stowed away as an emergency back up to our regular LPG system. There was always some mineral spirits aboard to burn in it. Other possibilities include a camper stove, Sterno and, in Europe, Camping Gaz. Also, I carried a single-burner electric hot plate that saved on propane use when we were dockside with shore power available.

Refrigeration

Refrigeration—to have or not to have—is sometimes a tough decision. You can live and cruise without it. A good quality unit is expensive to buy and install, and they're insatiable energy consumers. But, ah, a cold beer at the end of a hot day. Crisp vegetables at sea. Dairy products lasting for weeks, frozen foods for months. And that which is prized above all things by the sun-parched mariner, the ice cube! An icebox may suffice for the weekend sailor, but block ice simply does not exist along much of the cruising sailor's route. So if you are going to cool your box, refrigeration is the only way.

There are two basic systems available for cooling a small boat's refrigerator box. One is a holdover system, which circulates refrigerant gas pumped by a compressor through tubing inside a holding plate or holdover plate. The refrigerant freezes a solution in the tank that maintains the compartment temperature for extended periods when the system is not running. The other way to refrigerate is with an evaporative system, which circulates evaporating refrigerant gas through pipes to absorb and remove heat directly from the compartment.

The holdover system is usually the heavier duty, more expensive equipment. When the compressor pump that circulates the refrigerant is engine-driven, recharging the plate(s) may require running the engine as much as one to three hours every day. Just how much charging time is required for this depends primarily on the quantity and quality of the insulation around the box and on the ambient temperature of the air and seawater in which you're cruising. These engine-driven systems are popular among many veteran cruisers. However, most mechanics seem to agree that it is bad for a diesel engine to run a great deal without any load on it, as is the case when you're running the engine just to keep the refrigerator cooled down. Also, shattering the peace of a quiet lagoon by running an engine for hours everyday verges on sacrilege, if you ask me. And as if that weren't enough, all that extra engine time can burn up a lot of precious diesel fuel on a long ocean crossing.

Alternatively, there are the less expensive, nearly silent evaporative systems, their small compressors powered by a 12-volt motor, such as the popular Adler-Barbour models. A relatively new arrival is the Cooler-erator brand icebox conversion kits, designed for use in recreational boats where low-voltage, efficient refrigeration is desired. The Cooler-ator is an easily installed thermo-electric air cooler that only draws about 3 amps. It will refrigerate and can extend the life of block ice by several days. You generally get what you pay for, and while these lighter units do refrigerate without running the ship's engine, they don't freeze much more than a tray of ice cubes. Nor do they lend themselves to being repaired abroad.

A third option is powering a holdover system's compressor pump with a powerful 12-volt motor rather than by a belt off the ship's engine. On my own boat, I installed a heavy duty Grunert Mariner refrigerator/freezer. It's built to last (and to be repaired) and uses a cold plate that could freeze a brontosaurus. SPARROW's wind and solar recharging systems kept the dedicated refrigerator batteries charged much of the time, coping with the unit's 60-to-80 amp-hour daily power consumption. So I didn't have to run the engine every day to have excellent refrigeration.

To prevent battery drainage, the unit I had was designed to cycle on only while the engine was running, but this safeguard can be by-passed. This is what I did, so that I could control when it switched on, either automatically or manually. SPARROW's unit had only one large freezer plate that kept everything in the freezer compartment (about half of the divided, 9 cubic foot box) frozen solid, while transferring ample cooling through the mica-faced plywood partition into the other, refrigerator half of the box. There are small, battery-powered fans you can install in the refrigerator/freezer to help keep tempera-tures uniform, or to transfer cooling from freezer to fridge, but this wasn't necessary in my installation. This set-up provided me with ex-cellent refrigeration without the need to run the engine. Alternatively, you can install a freezer plate in the freezer, and a refrigeration plate in the refrigerator compartment.

Whatever refrigeration system you choose to install, it's likely to be the biggest energy consumer on the boat. If you use an engine-driven compressor unit, plan to provide for that by expecting excessive engine running time, or by installing a small, dedicated engine (such as a gen-set) to drive the compressor pump. Or you can beef up the electrical system's storage and charging capability, as I did, to cope with the drain of an electrically driven refrigerator compressor. We'll explore this last avenue in greater detail in Chapter 13.

Barbecue

A barbecue on the boat isn't as frivolous as it may first appear. A stainless steel, stern rail-mounted barbecue grill is truly an extension of the belowdecks galley. It makes an occasion out of a meal, provides a break for the galley slave, and cooks a meal without heating up the cabin, a big asset in the tropics. Fish cooked below will usually leave an odor, but not when grilled topsides. A barbecue is also a great back-up unit in case the galley stove ever quits working.

If you use propane for your ship's stove, use it also for the grill. Wet charcoal is said to be a fire hazard, capable of combusting spontaneously. If you use charcoal, store it in watertight containers and never put it away damp. Charcoal lighter fluid should be stowed carefully in a topside locker or deck box.

Galley Sink and Storage

Most sailors prefer double stainless steel sinks in the galley, deep ones to contain sloshing water underway. One sink is for washing; the other for rinsing or for leaving rinsed dishes to drip dry. Because sink bottom drains are sometimes barely above the outside sea level, the drain hose may stay full of dirty water all the time and can develop an odor. On SPARROW, I plumbed the sinks' drain through a small Whale Gusher foot pump, then overboard through the sink drain's seacock. I pumped out dishwater using one foot while I washed up, keeping both hands free for scrubbing, and then pumped the hose dry when I was through. The pump had a one-way valve, so water couldn't back up into the hose from the outside.

In the galley cabinets the dishes, bowls and cups call for secure storage. You don't want all that stuff clattering and rattling whenever the boat moves. Breakable china, wine glasses and the like are safest in a cupboard rack specially designed to fit and hold them securely.

Notes: A spice rack on a bulkhead is neat, homey and functional. Fiddle rails around the galley counters help keep meals off the cabin sole. So does dishware with non-skid bottoms.

Provisioning and Food Storage

Good food adds to the pleasure of life, especially the cruising life. There's no need to switch from land fare to Saltines and Spam afloat. In fact, this may be a good time to clean up your act and cut out some of the junk food with which you've been polluting your body.

Familiar foods are often hard to find in foreign countries. To eat well while voyaging you've got to plan ahead. Begin by noting the quantities of regular food items you normally consume per week or per month prior to going cruising. Then multiply those figures to come up with a long-term consumption estimate. Finally, substitute comparable items as necessary. For example, some perishable foods will have to be replaced by dehydrated, canned, smoked, or otherwise preserved equivalents from time to time.

When I provision, I like to stock a six-month to one-year supply of basic non-perishables aboard my boat, especially staples like rice, beans, grains for making flour, dried fruits, canned foods, sprouting seeds (a great way to always have fresh salads aboard), etc. You may get a discounted price from your local grocer if you explain that you're purchasing such a quantity of food: large sacks of flour, rice and beans, whole cases of peanut butter and canned tuna, and so on. You may do even better shopping at a bulk food store like Sam's Club, where food is sold by the case. I find health food stores often cooperate about pricing for quantity, and little wonder. You can spend several thousand dollars stocking the boat with a year's supply of non-perishable foods. Just remember, it'll pay off handsomely in the long run in both savings and nutrition.

If your boat does not have refrigeration, buy small size containers of those foods requiring refrigeration after opening, like mayonnaise, so that you will finish the contents before they spoil. Of course, fresh produce and other perishables must be re-stocked at every opportunity en route. Also, you might as well resolve yourself to making allowances and substitutions for some things common at home, but unavailable elsewhere.

The following are some items to stock up on in the United States due to their unavailability or high cost elsewhere: curry powder, chili powder, oregano, paprika, poultry and seafood seasonings, catsup, mayonnaise, peanut butter, popcorn, toilet paper, feminine hygiene products, cosmetics, razor blades, shampoo, pins and needles, rags, camera film, fishing gear, and self sealing plastic food storage bags.

Also, load up on Ecover brand liquid soap. I first discovered Ecover aboard a Greenpeace ship I was docked next to in Mallorca. Ecover is an environmentally safe, totally biodegradable, phosphate-free all purpose soap that lathers in seawater as well as in fresh. If you don't find it for sale locally, you might find it at, or order it through, a good health store or on the Internet at www.ecover.com. Since it works in salt water, it is precious indeed for washing dishes, bodies, hair, clothing and everything else in seawater when fresh water must be conserved for drinking.

Storing bulk food items, like a 50-lb. sack of rice, may seem daunting at first. Some smart cruisers collect those white plastic buckets with tight fitting lids that you see thrown out behind restaurants all the time, but ask the chef's permission first. I found some large, discarded commercial plastic olive jars with gasketed, screw-on lids behind a Greek delicatessen in Miami. Any of these, scrubbed clean and lined with a plastic trash bag (heavy-duty trash compactor bags are better), make ideal food storage containers. Pour in the rice or whatever you're storing, twist the bag closed, secure the lid, and label the container. Some foods will keep for years this way. Put a few whole bay leaves into containers of bulk grains, beans, seeds and rice to discourage weevils.

When storing canned goods, remove the paper labels, write the contents on the lid with a grease pencil, and varnish or lacquer the can. This will keep the paper labels out of the bilge pump, identify the food item long after labels would have come off anyway, and keep the cans from rusting. Glass bottles are best stored in the bilges where they can't fall. I stash my bottled beer and wine in a waterproof river rafting duffel bag bought at a sporting goods shop, to keep any bilge water off. A humble wine cellar to be sure, but it works. By the way, a limited selection of wine is also available in waxed box containers.

Food provisioning is lots of work, but it's exciting, too. It means you're almost ready to cast off.

Other Helpful Hints

- If the galley stretches along one side of the cabin, the cook is going to have a heck of a time using it when the boat is heeled over. Far preferable is a U-shaped layout that encloses the cook on three sides.

- You'll find plenty of uses for assorted plastic food containers with lids. They're available at most supermarkets and department stores. A good supply of plastic food storage bags is also handy.

- Make sure your galley utensils are stainless steel or plastic. Any ferrous metal will rust at sea. Pack at least one good fish fillet knife and a sharpening stone or tool.

- Stainless steel pots and pans that stack, with detachable handles, will permit you to store a complete set in a small space, and can be used in the oven as well as on stovetop burners. A stainless steel pressure cooker is a very good investment. It'll reduce both cooking time and stove fuel consumption. A stainless steel wok may be useful, too.

- A moveable cutting board is useful on deck for filleting fish.

- A thermos bottle keeps soup, coffee, tea, etc. warm for the night watch.

- Consider carrying a hand-operated or electric grain grinder to make bread from scratch. There are times when bread just cannot be purchased. Whole grain, ground as needed, will keep longer and is more nutritious than stored flour.

- Use a rubber cook's apron whenever you're cooking underway. It will deflect spilled scalding water, a real danger in the cruising galley.

- Don't forget to bring clothespins.

Trash

Too many of the world's most beautiful spots—the bluest lagoons, the whitest beaches, the farthest oceans—are polluted with man's garbage. Trash disposal is a serious global environmental issue of particular concern to the cruising sailor.

It is now illegal (it always was immoral) to throw plastic into the sea. We have a duty to stash our trash aboard until we can dispose of it properly ashore. For some, this suggests using a trash compactor, either installed or portable and hand-operated. For most, it means securing double-bagged trash on the after-deck or in a lazarette locker until we reach port. Outside of harbors, most cruisers toss food scraps overboard. There's no harm to that, but if you like to swim off the boat offshore, watch out for sharks that may follow the food trail. On long passages, some sailors jettison all biodegradable trash, and sink bottles and cans by filling them with seawater before tossing them. Others save all the garbage for port, as a matter of conscience. Anyone who pollutes our oceans with plastic, oil or chemicals ought to get thirty lashes. On second thought, make it forty.

The fixed rules are: offshore, crush and stow all plastic trash. Always pour waste oil and chemicals into a dedicated container. In port, never throw anything overboard.

Chapter 11

⌒⌒

Fresh Water

Rain Catchers

Getting clean, fresh water from shoreside facilities while cruising can range from inconvenient to expensive to impossible. One traditional way to replenish the ship's water supply is by catching rainwater. You can design all your boat awnings to double as rain catchers, with hose fittings (plastic 3/4" thru-hull fittings work well) or cloth funnels sewn into them to which hoses are clamped when it rains (see Figure 18). These channel the collected water directly into water tanks and jugs. Additional collection cloths can be strung about along the side decks or the foredeck.

The hoisted mainsail becomes an excellent water catcher, once rinsed clean of salt, by taking up on the topping lift to form a sail scoop that funnels water to the gooseneck where it's collected in a bucket. Stringing your sail cover upside down beneath the boom is another trick. On some boats, you can simply stop up the deck scuppers once the decks are rinsed clean and salt-free, and in calm to moderate seas let all that beautiful rain just pour into the water tank deck fills.

Once, while I was anchored out in the Abacos aboard the ketch AUTANT, I topped off my nearly empty tanks during a heavy downpour. I was feeling very pleased with myself until, afterwards, I discovered all the cinders and ash I'd collected at the same time. It seems there had recently been a big brush fire on the island across the bay to

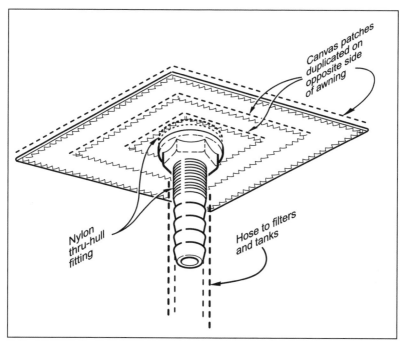

Figure 18: A removable plastic hose fitting installed through a reinforcing patch can turn any awning into an effective rain catcher. Just attach a length of hose to funnel the water directly into a water tank deck fitting.

windward. The breeze picked up the smoke and ash, carrying it downwind, and the rain dumped the debris on me and my great rain collection system, at anchor miles away. The water had a raunchy, burnt taste. What a chore it was emptying and cleaning the tanks! The moral is, inspect and taste the first bucket-full of collected water before you feed it into your tanks. In general, I avoid collecting rain in, near or downwind of a city. Rain can carry air pollutants with it.

Hot Water

Today, most boat manufacturers install water heaters that work both from dockside electricity and, through a heat exchanger, from running the engine. However, this isn't very useful to the average cruising sailor, who tries to minimize both situations. That is, he tends to anchor out most of the time, and he endeavors to run the engine as little as possible. So, a better alternative is a propane hot-water-on-demand heater like the stainless steel model made by Wolter. It is very efficient, heating only the water being used. Though my Wolter water heater was mounted in the head, it also heated the water for the galley sink.

There are other, less expensive alternatives. You can always heat water (salt or fresh) on the stove for a sponge bath when it's cold out. Then there's the popular Sun Shower, a black plastic bag of sun-heated water, which works just fine in warm, sunny weather. A variation of this is a black 3- to 5-gallon can, mounted on deck above the head, gravity fed below to provide an indoor shower. If you want the high tech version, use a clean, commercial insecticide spray can. After heating in the sun it can be pressurized by hand pumping and used on deck or in the head belowdecks. Flat black is the most heat absorbent color. However you do it, include a hot shower in your accommodations. You and your crew deserve it.

Aboard boats that do not have a watermaker, potable water is for drinking only during long ocean passages. So bathing in seawater is the rule. Bucket bathing is actually kind of fun in warm weather. Afterwards, if you can afford a cup or two of fresh water for a final rinse to remove the salt, you'll feel perfectly clean.

Watermakers

I enjoyed long, luxurious fresh water showers everyday of my two Atlantic crossings aboard SPARROW, yet I collected no rainwater. Still, I arrived on the other side with full water tanks. I owed this miracle to a small, efficient, 12-volt watermaker. PUR Watermakers manufactures a series of 12-volt desalinator watermakers capable of producing from 1.5 to 6.7 gallons per hour, depending on the model. These compact units fit aboard any sailboat, draw only a few amps, and make excellent-tasting fresh water, so there's always plenty—enough even for fresh showers in mid-ocean. (Blasphemy, cry the old salts! Wonderful, say I!) I suggest you plumb your watermaker directly into the ship's smaller water tank, leaving the second tank untouched, full and in reserve until port is made.

For bigger boats and budgets, there are many larger watermakers available that are powered by the generator. Some are capable of making hundreds of gallons per hour, although what a cruising couple would do with that much water is beyond me.

Of all the equipment and gadgets we pack onto our boats these days, a watermaker is the only one that will sustain life. The PUR units can also be operated manually, and the same manufacturer makes smaller handheld, hand-operated units perfect for the liferaft survival kit. I rate these watermakers high on the valuable equipment list for ocean voyaging, and for just hanging out in remote islands where drinking water is scarce or non-existent.

Tankage

Tanks in modern yachts are generally made of stainless steel or aluminum, and sometimes of heavy-duty plastic for the holding tanks. Alternatively, some or all of the tanks may be *integral,* formed on two or more sides by the vessel's hull. If the water tanks are metal, they should be made of stainless steel. Fuel tanks and metal holding tanks, on the other hand, are best made of aluminum because diesel fuel and holding tank sewage can deteriorate stainless steel welds, eventually resulting in leaks.

You'll want inspection ports to access all the ship's tanks for cleaning. Also, have an easy way to check tank levels. You can install electric sensors and gauges, but they seem to break a lot. A simple sight gauge—clear hose mounted vertically with each end plumbed into the tank—will do the job as well, and last longer. Simpler still is a dipstick. Having at least two separate water tanks, each with its own shut-off valve, will help protect against contamination or loss of your entire supply of drinking water. If water is carried in integral fiberglass tanks, coat them if possible with epoxy inside to avoid having water that tastes of resin. Any metal tank exteriors, even stainless steel, are best epoxy coated to increase their life expectancy. Always carry at least one spare 5-gallon jerrycan of diesel fuel, as well as a couple of jugs of spare water kept with the survival kit.

A quick way to increase a boat's tankage capacity is with collapsible *water tanks*. These large bags are made of rubber or plastic and can be installed in almost any available space, as low in the hull as possible. My own experience with collapsible water tanks is limited, but what I have heard and seen isn't encouraging. I think they're prone to chafing and leaking. I'd much sooner invest in a watermaker than in makeshift extra water tankage. On a small vessel, you can stash lots of 2-liter plastic bottles in little nooks all over the boat to increase your total water carrying capacity.

Adding just a little chlorine to tank water, whatever its source, retards bacteria and algae growth. A good water filter for the drinking water removes the chlorine taste. In diesel fuel tanks use an additive to prevent growth of fungus, which can contaminate the entire fuel system and damage the engine. However, be sure to use an additive that does not contain alcohol, which degrades plastic fuel system parts.

Plumbing Tips

Install an in line, heavy-duty water filter/purifier to remove impurities and unpleasant taste from the water you use for cooking and drinking. This filtered water will have its own tap in the galley, pressurized from the ship's water pressure pump or from a dedicated manual hand or foot pump. You'll find you use it constantly and you'll appreciate the improved water. You will have to replace the filter cartridge annually, so order a couple of spares ahead of time if you're going abroad.

Ideally, the galley will have deep, double stainless steel sinks. If you have a problem with seawater coming up into the galley sink when the boat's heeled over, you can plumb the sink drain through a foot pump. It will guarantee you a dry sink under all conditions. Though this requires that your foot is simultaneously pumping water out as you're running water into the sink, it soon becomes such a habit that you don't even notice you're doing it.

Foot pumps are easier to use than hand pumps for drawing water manually because they leave your hands free. There ought to be one each for salt and fresh water in the galley, and perhaps one for fresh water in the head sink. The manual fresh water pumps are really just a back-up system in case the boat's 12-volt pressure water system fails, but they're important when that happens. Incidentally, if your pressure water system doesn't include an accumulator tank, consider installing one. An accumulator tank maintains an even pressure in the system and prevents the electric pump from cycling excessively.

If you plan to be dockside often, install a deck fitting to which a garden hose attaches, for running city water directly into your fresh water system. This will save unnecessary wear and tear on the electric water pump. However, city water pressure is inconsistent and often too high for a boat's plumbing system. There's a very real danger it'll blow out a hose or fitting aboard and flood—even sink—the boat right at the dock. A gadget called a constant pressure reducer, installed at the garden hose connection, will keep the pressure within safe limits inside the boat. They're available from plumbing or RV supply stores. Still, it's wise to shut off the city water at the dock spigot whenever you're leaving the boat.

Chapter 12

~~~

Navigation, Electronics and Communication

In the days of yore, during the Golden Age of Sail, much was made of the mystical art of navigation. An exaggerated ceremony was performed daily aboard ship by the officers for the benefit of the crew, who were often kept from mutiny solely by the fact that none among them could navigate. Thus, they relied entirely on the Captain and the First Mate for this, and a balance of power was maintained at sea.

Today there is, hopefully, little threat of mutiny aboard our small ships, and the secrets of the art of navigation have become available to all who care to learn. GPS has demoted the sextant to a back-up system, albeit still an essential one. The bullhorns, signal flags and signal lanterns of yesteryear have been replaced by radios, telephones and e-mail. Times have changed for the better.

Now, let's consider some outfitting ideas to make it even easier to navigate and communicate aboard the modern cruising sailboat.

Navigation Station

In a very small sailboat, the dinette table may have to double as the navigator's chart table, but most cruising boats today have a dedicated navigation station and this is preferable. The navigator is likely to spend a fair amount of time there while under way, so it needs to be reasonably comfortable and designed so that he and his tools stay put no matter how the boat is heeling or rocking. In any case, assign an area for navigating, with places for the tools of the craft such as charts, books, manuals, tables, worksheets, divider and parallels, protractor if you use one, pencils, sharpener, etc.

Mount a chronometer, a very accurate clock or watch, where it can be easily seen. The chronometer is set to Zulu (Greenwich Mean Time or Coordinated Universal Time) and checked for accuracy against a radio time signal regularly. In addition, a nav station alarm clock set to local time is handy offshore to signal watch changes and times for taking sights or otherwise fixing and logging your position at sea.

The placement of the electronics in the navigation station takes some thoughtful planning. In general, displays for the GPS, the radar, and the chart plotter, if you have them, should be right in front of the navigator's seat, since he will want to look at these most often. Because of a convenient positioning of the nav table on my boat, SPARROW, these instruments were also facing the quarter berth directly aft, where I preferred to sleep while offshore, so I could glean basic information at a glance without getting out of bed (see Figure 19). These primary displays were also angled slightly toward the companionway, enabling me to see them easily from the helm. I had to build a small shelf over part of the nav table, from which the radar screen was suspended, to accomplish this very functional arrangement. If your boat's configuration does not permit this, you can install repeaters in the cockpit, preferably under the dodger.

Radios can be almost anywhere around the nav station, but try to place the VHF radiotelephone within reach of the companionway. You'll often want to use it while standing in the cockpit. (You can install a separate VHF radio in the cockpit if you like.) Depth, speed and wind repeaters belowdecks can also be off to the side of the nav station, being less vital to route planning and position plotting.

Unfortunately, many manufacturers (SPARROW's included) install the ships electrical panel smack in the middle of the navigation station area. This takes up valuable space with switches and meters that could

Figure 19: SPARROW's nav station arrangement was functional, if not ideal. The breaker panel should have been located somewhere else.

just as well be elsewhere in the cabin, preferably where spray from the companionway cannot reach them.

We'll be talking more about on board computers. For now, suffice it to say that computers are becoming an integral part of many modern nav stations, just as they are playing an increasing role in many lives ashore, and you may want to allocate space for one at your chart table. There are lots of ways to interface other systems with a computer, such as combining the Single Sideband radio with the computer to receive weatherfax and e-mail, and connecting the computer to a cell or satellite phone for Internet connection.

In fact, to the extent that you are so inclined, you can turn over many of the ship's functions, particularly navigational, to a computer. But consider this. I was sitting at my nav table on a beautiful reach off the Canary Islands once, bound toward the West Indies and writing on my laptop. The companionway hatch was open to let in the fine weather. A wavelet crested off the ship's quarter and spat a one-cup dollop of sea-water that arched in through the open hatch directly onto the keyboard of my computer. It would have been comical except it immediately destroyed my laptop and I had to do without until I arrived on the other side of the Atlantic Ocean. Meanwhile, I had to do my writing with pen and paper, and do without weatherfax and other computer functions entirely. If your nav station is adjacent to the companionway, as many are, consider rigging a clear plastic shower curtain while offshore to prevent spray from dousing your electronics. And remember, all this gadgetry is fine and fun, but it will fail at the worst possible time. Be sure you can operate and navigate without the electronics.

One more note: Weather and other informational radio broadcasts often come in too fast and too fuzzy offshore for taking notes. A small cassette tape recorder is useful for recording these to play back again.

Celestial Navigation Tools

It's foolish to go to sea without the ability and the tools to navigate by the sun, moon, stars and planets. Electronic navigation just doesn't provide the same gratification as does celestial navigation. More to the point, electronics, which we'll discuss in some detail a bit further on, can and do break. So, before buying the GPS, the programmed calculators and the computers, the following instruments should be on board any bluewater cruising sailboat:

- Sextant, calibrated

- Spare sextant, plastic (possibly stowed in the Abandon Ship kit)

- Chronometer with measured rate of change

- Stopwatch on a lanyard (or wrist watch set precisely to GMT)

- Short wave radio receiver for time signals

- Star finder

- Pencils #2

- Pencil sharpener

- Parallel rulers (or similar device)

- Dividers and compass

- Plain paper or printed worksheets

- Current nautical almanac

- Sight Reduction Tables for the latitudes of the voyage

- Universal plotting sheets

Books and Charts For Traditional Navigation

There are numerous texts and reference books available to aid the ocean navigator. The following represent a few of the publications most useful to the cruising sailor:

- *Reed's Nautical Almanac and Coast Pilot*, current regional issue

- *Sight Reduction Tables* for all latitudes and for selected stars, published by the Defense Mapping Agency Hydrographic Center

- *Piloting, Seamanship, and Small Boat Handling* by Charles F. Chapman

- *Celestial Navigation in a Nutshell* by Hewitt Schlereth, *Self Taught Navigation* by Robert Y. Kittredge, *A Star to Steer Her By* by Edward J. Bergin (or similar easy-to-follow book on how to navigate with a sextant)

- *World Cruising Routes* by Jimmy Cornell

- *Ocean Passages of the World*, a British Admiralty publication

- Pilot Charts for the planned cruise area

- Regional cruising guide books

- Sailing Directions and Coast Pilots as need dictates

- Catalogs of nautical charts and publications

- Large and small-scale charts (use chart kits when available) of areas you intend to cruise, preferably published by the country most influential in that region (such as French charts for Polynesia). In America, The Better Boating Association, Inc. publishes excellent, money-saving chart kits for much of the United States, the Bahamas, and the Virgin Islands.

Most cruising sailors have neither the budget nor the storage space to stock a truly complete set of new charts for an extended cruise. The Mediterranean region alone could require literally hundreds of small scale, large scale, and harbor charts costing thousands of dollars. Fortunately, there are ways to save both money and space while acquiring all the navigational data you need, especially in popular cruising areas.

Small-scale charts, those covering a relatively large area, provide the overview necessary for route planning. Less than two dozen can cover the whole Med, and even fewer the Caribbean Sea. These are then supplemented with regional cruising guidebooks, which contain local sailing directions and many large-scale and harbor charts. A good guidebook can save you from having to buy many large-scale charts and often provides terrific local knowledge to boot, like how to clear in, who sells fresh bread, and where to go dancing—all valuable information.

Today, buying even a basic set of new charts is an expensive proposition. So, when I meet a fellow cruiser who has charts I know I'm going to need soon, I sometimes ask if I may borrow them to photocopy. In most cities, you can find an architectural supply store with a photocopy machine large enough to duplicate full-size nautical charts. The cost is usually a few dollars per copy. Some machines can even reduce copies down to two-thirds the size of the original. This makes a handy size chart for a yacht's chart table, as long as you can still read it easily.

Another source of cut-rate charts is through the Seven Seas

Cruising Association (Fort Lauderdale, Florida). They and similar or-
ganizations publish a list of members with used charts to sell or swap.
Nautical Internet chat groups and bulletin boards are another possible
place to find used charts.

Now, I'm going to let you in on a real cruiser's trick. Ships—
freighters, tankers, and cruise ships—replace their charts regularly.
Their insurance requires it. These slightly used charts are perfectly
good for our purposes, yet the ships' officers generally throw them
away. Just pay a visit to the next ship you see in port, ask to speak to
the captain or to the officer in charge regarding navigational information, and then ask him if they've got any outdated charts they no
longer need. You just may be rewarded with a stack of excellent nautical charts for free. One sailor I know received nearly two hundred
free charts from one ship, then wound up being invited to dinner
aboard with the captain.

Of course, swapping charts with other cruising sailors is an ongoing affair, especially at crossroads like Gibraltar and Panama. Check
the marina and pub bulletin boards.

Basic Electronics

Electronics for the private yacht have really come of age. You can interface the speed/log, the fluxgate compass and the GPS with the
computer, which sends directions to the autopilot. Enter the waypoints
into the system, then all you need is a radio remote control unit,
interfaced through the Single Sideband radio, and you could just send
the boat off without you. Stay home and watch it all on a video screen.
Just think of it! No seasickness; no more wet, sleepless nights. Later,
you can fly to Bermuda and meet the boat there.

Of course, I'm just kidding. But really, it can get out of hand. Your
own budget and personal inclinations will determine how far you go
with this stuff. My order of priorities for circumnavigating is:

- Autopilot. First and foremost! To steer the boat so that you
  don't have to. Carry two if you can, one to be used while the

other is off being repaired. At least, carry complete spare parts and a repairman's manual.

- VHF (Very High Frequency) radio. For short-range ship to ship and ship to shore communication. All-band frequencies are necessary for international cruising.

- GPS (Global Positioning System). For determining your latitude and longitude. Although you'll have sextants to back it up, you just can't beat a GPS for easy and accurate fixes. I'd carry a spare, as well.

- Depthsounder. To constantly read the water's depth beneath your boat. Consider it necessary equipment.

- Radar. For finding and reading landmasses, and for sighting ships and other above-water obstructions. You'll want at least a 16-mile range, with a perimeter alarm.

- SSB (Single Sideband) radio and/or ham radio. For long range informational, social, safety, and emergency communication, ship to ship and ship to shore.

- Weatherfax. For current weather maps and text reports. Either purchase it as a unit, or else obtain it by interfacing the SSB or ham radio with an on board computer.

- Computer. For multiple functions and for fun. Not necessary for cruising, but may be necessary for living, depending on how hooked you are.

- Omni-directional radar detector. To warn of approaching ships, but it only works if they have their radar turned on at sea, which they often do not. Maybe it's better than nothing if you do not have a radar with perimeter alarm on your boat.

- Knot meter (speed/log). Not essential, but useful for DR and for bragging about how fast you were going.

- Electronic wind speed and direction indicators. To tell you where the wind is blowing from and how hard, as if you didn't know. It's amusing, but certainly not necessary.

- RDF (Radio Direction Finder). Pinpoints the source direction of a radio signal. A helpful tool for the traditional navigator. However, except as a back-up system, the RDF is of little use today aboard a boat equipped with GPS.

Of course, by the time you get all this equipment installed and operational, it's already becoming obsolete. Every year the units get smaller, better and cheaper. Therefore, electronics should be among the last items to be purchased and installed for your cruise.

Remember, you *must* be able to navigate using a sextant before you venture offshore. All of the above electronics are merely conveniences, to be used with discretion by a competent navigator. Many years ago, I learned celestial navigation quickly and inexpensively from a delightful, skinny little book titled *Self Taught Navigation* by Robert Y. Kittredge. It may be out of print now, but there are other how-to-navigate books on the shelves of most marine bookstores. The thin ones are generally best for starters. If you're not already proficient at celestial navigation, invest in such a book and learn this simple, over-dramatized skill, without using calculators and computer programs, while you're shaking down your boat. Then, and only then, treat yourself to GPS.

Computers

The decision whether or not to have a computer on a sailboat is a purely personal one. You certainly don't need it to go cruising, but if you're already hooked on computers and can't imagine living without one, then go for it. Computers are every bit as functional and entertaining afloat as they are ashore, although Internet and e-mail access may be more difficult and more costly.

Today's compact laptops are powerful enough to rival the capabilities of many bigger desktop units. Certainly, a laptop will fit aboard more readily. Laptop computers run on DC (Direct Current) electricity, but may require a bit more than the 12- to 13-volts available from your boat's battery bank. There are DC (battery-powered) printers available, too, some of which require a small converter to lower the ship's 12-volt DC to 9-volt DC. However, to be able to use all computers and printers, and many of the computer accessories and features available to land-based users, you'll need a power inverter on your boat to provide AC electricity when away from the dock. This is the smart way to do it. Then you can simply plug everything in using the equipments' standard adapters, just like on shore. If you're only installing an inverter to provide this small amount of power, there are inexpensive units available at any good RV or automotive store.

A computer can store countless charts, the entire nautical almanac series for the next century, star finders, piloting information such as light lists, tides and currents, performance programs, the ship's log and family games. It makes letter writing a snap. If you have the program and the cable, your computer can be interfaced with the SSB to receive weatherfax, and to send and receive fax and e-mail messages. You can go online and surf the world wide web while you're surfing down the face of a following sea in mid-ocean, hooking up to the telephone system from your vessel via SSB and ham radio stations, or via satellite telephone.

Today, computerized chart kits are readily available on disks and CDs. For cruising purposes, I recommend using only those electronic charts that are identical reproductions of standard paper nautical charts, i.e. digitalized or raster-scanned charts. Computerized charts have several advantages over traditional printed charts: (1) they take up virtually no space aboard your boat; (2) you can zoom in on and enlarge the chart section you need; (3) the computer can be interfaced with the GPS and/or the radar to constantly display your vessel's relative position; (4) many computerized charts (and light lists) can be instantly and completely updated with computerized Notice to Mariners updates; (5) you can do all route planning, plotting and editing on computer and, through an autopilot interface, allow the computer to "steer" the selected course.

The disadvantages of computerized charts are: (1) you must first have a computer capable of supporting the chart program; (2) computerized charts take up a great deal of disk space, even when they're compressed; (3) there are gaps in many of the chart catalogs for the areas of the world that are less traveled, just the places that some of us want to go; (4) being a new industry, competing computerized chart manufacturers have not yet standardized their programs. Some of them will go the way of the 8-track music cassette; you could wind up investing in a future dinosaur; (5) you absolutely must have paper charts aboard covering your entire passage in addition to the computerized charts (and you also still need to carry all other basic navigational and plotting tools aboard), because when the computer stops working you'll need to navigate the old fashioned way or else risk being totally lost out there. Therefore, do not bother to invest in any computerized chart program that does not have full print capability, allowing you to print out hard copies of every nautical chart you might possibly need for any given passage before you set sail. Given that, however, I think some level of computerized charting makes sense if you can afford it.

Computerized charting is a relatively new technology that is evolving rapidly. The programs and systems differ greatly in capabilities and prices. Anything specific I write on the subject today is likely to be dated information by the time you read this. Do some research and some shopping around before you buy. As is often the case, current or recent issues of boating magazines, manufacturer's boat show exhibits, marine chandleries, online chat groups and fellow boaters are your best sources of up-to-the-minute comparative information.

Communications

The whole field of computer technology and wireless communication is undergoing a revolution, both on- and offshore. The companies, and the systems and equipment they provide, are legion; their products, capabilities and costs vary widely and change continuously. There is little standardization, so many systems and devices are incompatible with one another. Brand names come and go, manufacturers change and merge, prices rise and fall.

For all these reasons, I can only offer a general overview of what's available at the present time. In addition to magazines, boat shows and other sailors' input, a patient, knowledgeable marine electronics salesperson may be an invaluable ally for sorting through and explaining the many systems and combinations available to you and what will serve you best based on your personal needs, your cruising plans and your budget.

VHF and Cell Phones

The VHF radio has long been the mainstay of communications between boats, and between boats and shore stations, within the limits of its range. Transmitting via a masthead antenna with 25 watts of power, the commercial VHF typically has a line-of-sight range of around 25 miles, but can sometimes reach farther depending in part on conditions and topography. Handheld VHF radios, with only 1 to 5 watts output, are useful for very short range communicating only.

Along the U.S. coasts, at some islands in the West Indies, and in many other regions around the world you can often make phone calls from the boat using your VHF radio, albeit less privately than with a telephone. To do so, you have to contact a shore-based marine operator. The most prevalent marine operator in the United States today is Maritel, which covers the East and Gulf coasts almost completely, but at this time provides only partial coverage on the West Coast.

When coastal cruising in the U.S., and increasingly in the West Indies, Central and South America and the Pacific Basin, the common cellular telephone used in the U.S. is a viable if sporadic means of communicating. Like a VHF radio, the cell phone employs a line-of-sight signal, so the higher the antenna, the longer will be the range within the limits of the unit's transmission power. In areas with good phone tower coverage and minimal traffic, ranges will increase. In other areas the operating range may be severely reduced or there may be no service at all.

You can increase the range of your on board cell phone by getting a booster kit or a more powerful *bag* phone. Bag phones are an evolution of the original briefcase cell phones, with a self-contained battery pack that enables the phone to transmit at 3 watts, as opposed to the handheld cell phone's modest 0.6 watts. By adding a marine cellular antenna mounted on the sailboat's masthead, you can often make and receive phone calls from 20 to 25 miles offshore and more.

You use a cell phone on your boat just as you would in a car. Depending on your service, you may have to switch to different regional carriers as you move if your system allows for or requires that. To use your American cell phone abroad, you may have to call your carrier in advance to arrange for the foreign service. European, African and Asian countries have a different cell phone system, called GSM, used with SIM cards, which are preprogrammed and programmable data chips. If you're going to be cruising in those waters for a while, you may want to buy a GSM phone.

Long Range Radios

Single Sideband (SSB) and ham radios have a range of up to several thousand miles. This is how mariners have communicated from mid-ocean for years, ship to ship and ship to shore, and still do. Marine operator stations worldwide can patch you into land-based telephone systems. The marine operator in the United States is Mobile Marine Radio (WLO), in Mobile, Alabama.

There are single sideband and ham radio nets covering most popular cruising areas around the world. These are chat groups organized mainly for socializing and sharing information, and to a lesser extent for emergency communications. The ham nets are generally more structured and more organized. The difference between ham and SSB are the frequencies they are permitted to use. In addition, ham radio operation requires a license that necessitates passing a written and a Morse code examination, keeping it a more exclusive group. SSB nets are less formal and, in the U.S., the license for SSB operation does not require an exam. For more information on SSB and ham radio installation and operation, pay a visit to an amateur radio shop.

If you do install a long range radiotelephone, you'll need to plan for proper grounding in order to be able to send a strong signal. When SPARROW was but a shell at the factory, the builder ran a 2" wide copper grounding strap completely around the inside of the hull and fiberglassed it in. This integral copper grounding strap, to which the ship's SSB or ham radios ground is attached, forms a ground plane that significantly enhances radio signal propagation. Some technicians feel that connecting the radio ground to an external plate, similar to the lightning ground dynaplate, is equally effective. Others say laying down a copper mesh in the bilges works well. But all agree that if you plan to use long range radios aboard, proper radio counterpoise will greatly improve performance. Consult with a marine radio expert for the best approach to use on your boat.

The other requirement for using your ham or SSB radio is a long, tune-able antenna. Sailboats have a natural antenna available in the backstay, but the stay wire must first be insulated. That means the wire is cut near both ends and reconnected with non-conductive fittings. Thus, the wire in between is electrically isolated from the rest of the rigging. The radio's antenna wire clamps to the backstay just above the lower insulator. (*Warning:* The lower insulator must be well above the height of people's reach from the deck so that they cannot accidentally touch the antenna section of the wire. If the antenna is touched while the radio is transmitting, a severe shock will result.) Stringing a separate antenna wire up the mast also works. Any antenna must be electronically tuned for various SSB and ham radio transmission frequencies, and this is accomplished with either a manual or an automatic antenna tuner. Again, don't hesitate to seek the advice of a professional for details of on board radio installations.

Satellite Telephones

Telephone communication via satellite is available from several providers at this time. Globalstar, Motient and Inmarsat Mini-M (and Inmarsat-C) are the key providers. Their coverage, capabilities, compatible equipment and rates vary and are forever evolving, but one or the other can hook you up almost anywhere in the world if that's what you want. Not only can you make and receive phone calls in mid-ocean, but on some systems and in some regions you can send and receive fax and log onto the Internet to browse and to send and receive e-mail. Contact the providers or a vendor to make valid, current comparisons and to determine which system best accommodates your needs and cruising grounds.

E-Mail

E-mail is a great way to stay in touch with friends, family and business while you're cruising. If you have a laptop computer with a modem, you can log onto your Internet service provider or e-mail carrier from any land phone, or you can set it up to connect through your cell or satellite phone, as well. Or you may opt for the PocketMail system or one of its competitors, such as MailStation and PostBox, for onshore and coastwise communicating. These devices are simpler, more compact and less expensive alternatives for sending and receiving e-mail, although at this time they do not handle e-mail attachments.

Offshore, your e-mail connection choices are single sideband and ham radio links, and satellite telephone systems. To utilize your long range radio for e-mail, you'll need an interface program and a radio modem connecting your computer to the radio. Globe Wireless offers this service using an international network of stations. Other services, such as the nonprofit group, SailMail, may offer lower prices but fewer stations. SSB and ham communications are affected by atmospheric conditions, time of day and even sunspots, so you can't always count on the connection.

Satellite phone carriers are providing more and more Internet capabilities and are often faster and more reliable than radio for sending and receiving e-mail. Right now, most of the systems are text only, but that will probably change in time. Inmarsat-C is a particular favorite among cruisers because it offers free weather and information broadcasts tailored regionally to your vessel's GPS location, and a Global Maritime Distress and Safety System (GMDSS) that is much more proactive than a plain EPIRB distress signal.

The equipment necessary for on board satellite communications, and for single sideband and ham radios, for that matter, runs into thousands of dollars. Like most electronics, these conveniences are likely to become smaller, better and cheaper as their popularity and sales volume increase. As usual, your budget and personal requirements will help you decide if and when this is a good investment for you.

Chapter 13

<c

The Integrated Energy System

An Optimum Electrical Power System
for the Cruising Sailboat

When a sailor forsakes dockside shore power for the wild blue yonder of the cruising world, his vessel becomes a self-sufficient living environment. It has to produce whatever energy is required to operate the various electrical and electronic accessories aboard. This entails periodically recharging the ship's storage batteries. Most sailors accomplish this by running the engine to drive the standard alternator. Boats with refrigeration, whether 12-volt or mechanical, run engines as much as three hours every day to keep the fridge and/or batteries topped off. To the long distance or liveaboard sailor, this translates into considerable fuel consumption and engine wear over the years. Running a large diesel engine without sufficient load on it will shorten its useful life, not to mention the noise it makes.

There are better alternatives to this common, inefficient method of deriving the ship's electrical energy from running the ship's main propulsion engine. The energy we need is available from the sun, wind, and water, and from more efficient fossil-fueled engines and bigger alternators. When combined in an integrated energy system, these contemporary sources can relieve the engine of double duty as a generator by providing 12-volt power for operating on board equipment, including refrigeration.

An *integrated energy system* for the cruising sailboat is simply a monitored combination of equipment that supplies, stores, and distributes ample electricity to meet the needs of the vessel. The four components of this optimum yacht electrical power system are the sources, the storage batteries, the distribution, and the monitors.

12-Volt Energy Sources

Solar Panels

The most fundamental, readily available source of energy on Earth is sunlight. The photovoltaic cell is an effective method for converting solar light energy into electrical energy. Multiple photocells (or solar cells) are laminated onto sheets of paper-thin stainless steel (for marine-grade solar panels) and sealed with a clear, protective coating of space-age polymers to form solar panels. Flat, lightweight, and durable, many of today's solar panels are well suited to use aboard boats.

There's a place and a need for one or more solar panels on nearly every cruising sailboat. Their function is to continuously and silently recharge the ship's batteries during hours of sunlight. For a vessel with minimal electrical gadgetry, located in a sunny region, this trickle charge may be all that's needed to keep batteries topped off. It's a valuable, virtually maintenance-free source of energy in an integrated energy system.

Solar panels are available today with either rigid or flexible housings. Rigid panels are marketed by a host of companies. They're usually between 1/2" and 1 1/2" thick and come framed in many rectangular sizes, the handiest being anywhere from one to three feet wide, and from two to four feet long. On a boat, they can be screwed flat on any clear deck area or cabin top, although they'll often need a bit of shimming to compensate for camber in the deck.

However, solar panels are most efficient when they're angled to face the sun directly. So it's a good idea to mount them in a manner that enables you to adjust the direction they face. At anchor, you could simply lean and lash a panel wherever it will get the most direct sunlight, but it's probably a better idea to gimbal-mount panels permanently so that they can pivot and/or tilt to optimize their angle to the sun. Stern rail mounting accomplishes this easily. Erecting reflectors to direct more sunlight onto the panel surface can enhance solar panel performance.

Flexible solar panels offer even more possibilities for sensible installations on a sailboat. They come in a variety of sizes ranging from one to eight square feet. Their chief advantage over rigid panels is their ability to mount smoothly on curved surfaces such as a cambered cabin trunk or deck, or on flexible surfaces like a dodger or a bimini top. They're lightweight and quite thin—about 1/4 inch—so they're never in the way. In addition, they can lash, snap or zip onto a sun awning, so while you're making shade you're also making electricity. On the down side, flexible panels may not be as efficient as their rigid counterparts. Check the rated watts when comparing solar panels' output.

The amount of electricity a solar panel produces depends primarily on the size of the panel and the directness of the sunlight striking it. Manufacturers tend to advertise absolute maximum amperage output of their products based on perfect, controlled conditions where blazing, unobstructed, perpendicular sunrays strike flat panels. The amperage output is then measured right at the panel.

In real life, however, the sky is rarely cloudless, nor the sun at maximum strength and declination. Rigging and spars will sometimes cast shadows, decreasing a panel's output. Also, on a boat the electricity must travel some distance through wiring and diodes before it trickles into the battery, further reducing amperage received. So when a panel is rated for, say, 3 amps (about 36 watts), it will actually yield a net average of 1.5 to 2.5 amps during the brightest part of the day. If a panel yields 2 amps for 5 hours a day, the batteries have received 10 amp-hours—enough to play the stereo and power your cabin lights that evening.

If you wire several panels together in series, the power output is multiplied. I saw a boat in Florida with eight 33-watt flexible solar panels mounted on the sun awning. That's 8 panels x 2 amps (approximate average output) = 16 amps x 5 (bright sun) hours per day = about 80 amp hours. That's enough amps to power a hefty 12-volt cold-plate refrigerator and freezer.

Wiring solar panels is simple. The wires pass inside the boat through a watertight fitting available at most marine stores. Some solar panels have a built-in diode, a device that allows current to flow in one direction only. If yours doesn't, then solder a diode in series in either of the two wires somewhere before the positive and negative wires connect to the corresponding battery bus terminals. A Schottky diode is recommended because of its low voltage drop. The diode will prevent batteries discharging through the panels after dark. For safety, you should install both an in-line fuse and an on/off switch between the solar panel and the distribution panel. You can also wire in an ammeter to monitor the amount of solar energy flowing into your batteries. Most competent marine electricians can help you set all this up.

Prices for marine-grade solar panels vary. Larger panels cost proportionally more than smaller ones. Expect to pay $300 to $500 or more for 1 ft. x 4 ft., 40-watt rigid panels, and as little as around $100 for small sizes that produce one amp or less.

Wind Generators

Harnessing the wind is nothing new to a sailor. With a wind generator, you can convert wind's kinetic energy into DC current for around-the-clock battery charging. Of course, this is a more productive energy source in regions of steady breezes, such as a tradewind belt.

A wind generator is a DC generator driven by a propeller. When the wind spins the prop fast enough, the unit produces a trickle charge ranging from an amp or two, up to 10 or 15 amps, depending on wind speed and the propeller and generator size. A full-size ship's wind generator in the Virgin Islands, where the tradewinds maintain a steady 15-knots much of the time, can easily produce 6 or 7 amps continuously, well over 100 amp-hours per 24-hour day. That's enough to power radios, lights, radar, television, and a 12-volt refrigerator/freezer.

Beware of manufacturers' specifications that promise amperage output in very light (5 to 7 knot) breezes. The measurements are taken at the generator output terminal and only indicate what a virtually dead battery might absorb in these wind conditions. For DC current to be accepted and stored, the source voltage must be higher than the voltage in the receiving battery. A wind generator may well be generating current in light airs, but at only 9, 10 or 11 volts. So no amps will go into a battery that's only partially discharged to, say, 12 volts, which is a typical on board scenario, and no charging will occur. Most of the large-bladed wind generators don't actually do much charging until the wind exceeds 10 knots. The small bladed, European-style units need a good deal more wind than that to charge batteries.

The popular American manufactured wind generators feature two- or three-blade propellers with diameters of four to five feet. These are hefty generators with relatively good light air performance. Some European designs are smaller in size, weight, and blade diameter, with multiple-bladed props. These are less productive in light breezes, but unlike the large models, they can be left running in very high winds.

There are several ways to mount a wind generator on a sailboat. It can be hoisted into the foretriangle area by a jib halyard while at anchor, and positioned by guys. This allows the unit to pivot and track wind shifts. But it must be taken down and stowed somewhere every time you want to get underway, so this installation is more practical aboard a vessel that tends to remain anchored for long periods of time. Some skippers mount their wind generator permanently on the forward side of a mizzenmast, which eliminates the set-up and tear down hassle, but will not allow the wind generator to pivot or face anything but a head wind. A bow pulpit mount is also rigid, with the added disadvantages of being vulnerable to damage and dangerous to crew.

The most effective solution is mounting on a pole. A pole-mounted wind generator, normally located at the stern, can pivot to face any wind shift as your boat sails back and forth at anchor or lies to a current or a dock. Best of all, it's always in position to operate, even under sail. When sailing close hauled, a stern pole-mounted unit is especially well powered, getting strong apparent wind funneled into it by the mainsail. The ability to operate underway makes the pole mount most valuable to cruising sailors, who need to keep their batteries charged during long offshore passages. Though this increases the boat's windage somewhat, it's not enough to matter to a sailboat loaded for cruising. An evolution of the pole mount arrangement is the bi-pole rig, discussed in Chapter 5.

A word of caution: The spinning blade of a wind generator

propeller can be very dangerous when mounted within reach. Brightly painted or reflective blade tips make the blade more noticeable to crewmembers.

Many wind generators come with some kind of over-speed governing device or brake to protect the unit against damage in very high winds. Otherwise, they must be manually shut down. In preparation for extreme wind conditions, they should be taken down altogether. Generally, they should not be left running when the boat is unattended for long periods. It may be worthwhile to wire your wind generator through a regulator to prevent overcharging of the batteries. Also, they need a diode, either installed in line or built into the unit itself, to prevent battery discharge in calm winds.

Wind generators, especially the larger units, create some noise and vibration. In moderate conditions, it's a whooshing sound that passes as unnoticed background noise. In high winds, it's often a louder fluttering, chopping, whirring noise. Some pole-mounted wind generators shudder momentarily when they pivot to track a wind shift, though a new generation of balanced props has largely eliminated this vibration on some brands.

Maintenance on wind generators is minimal. Wooden propeller blades need occasional painting or varnishing. Periodically, the brushes and bearings in the generator need replacing, just as in an automobile alternator. But for the most part, wind generators just keep on working, night and day, to keep your ship's batteries charged. After the initial cost of purchase, usually ranging from $800 to $2,000, your ship's electrical energy is as free as the wind.

Water Generators

Water generators can be a valuable addition to the cruising sailor's integrated energy system. They are the least common alternate energy source, perhaps because of the inevitable drag created by towing that extra propeller in the water—25 to 35 lbs. of drag at 6 knots. Or perhaps it's because most boats spend the majority of their time in anchorages rather than under sail.

A water generator is a DC generator activated by a propeller towed in the water. The prop is allowed to freewheel when the boat is underway. There are four basic ways to set this up, and then there are variations of these: (1) by trailing a propeller astern on a cable or braided line. The passing water spins the prop, which twists the cable. The cable turns the generator mounted on the stern rail. On some models the prop is attached to the generator and a cable tows the entire unit; (2) by mounting a style of water generator that looks like a small outboard motor. Its lower gear case and propeller are submerged; (3) by installing a dedicated propeller shaft through the hull of your boat, letting it freewheel when sailing to turn the generator; (4) by connecting a generator by way of a belt, bicycle chain, or gear drive to the ship's main prop shaft and allowing that to freewheel when sailing.

The trailing portion of the first, towed type may be damaged or taken by large fish. The latter two options require custom design and installation, and some transmissions may be damaged if you allow the ship's propeller to freewheel while sailing. Check the manufacturer specifications.

Many wind generators readily convert to water generators, propelled by the cable and prop method. In fact, wind and water generators are much the same in terms of cost and maintenance, being the same machine with different drives. Because the fluid coupling between water and propeller is much greater than between wind and propeller, water propulsion yields about double the amps per knot of speed, generating about 5 amps at 6 knots of boat speed. To get the same 5 amps from the wind requires about a 12-knot breeze. For a sailboat making an ocean passage, running down the trades at 6 knots or more, there's an extra 120 daily amp hours for the taking. On a cloudy day, on a dead run with little apparent wind, when the solar and wind energy just isn't coming through, the water generator will run everything aboard as long as you keep sailing.

Like the wind generator, the water generator must be manually shut off when your batteries are topped off. Or it can be wired through a regulator, eliminating this requirement.

Generators and alternators are very similar machines. Both produce DC current for charging batteries. Generators are more rugged than alternators; alternators are the more efficient of the two. If you'd like to build your own wind or water generator from an ordinary alternator, *The 12-Volt Doctor's Practical Handbook* by Ed Beyn describes how to do it.

Engine Alternators

The alternate energy sources we've discussed so far are all important ingredients in the integrated energy system. They will greatly reduce, if not entirely eliminate, the need to run the engine in order to charge batteries. But the main engine's alternator can and should be a ready source of electrical energy, particularly when you're running the engine to propel the boat anyway.

Most marine diesel engines come standard with too small an alternator to cope with the large capacity battery bank of the liveaboard cruising sailboat. It may well be that with solar, wind, and water energy sources, you often won't need more than a small alternator. However, in harbor conditions of overcast skies and light winds, the alternator becomes your only means of recharging the batteries away from the dock. So a more efficient system is worth considering.

For years now we've been hearing about switches that enable us to manually over-ride the alternator's regulator for quick-charging the batteries. One of the functions of the regulator is to control the voltage output of the alternator or generator by regulating the current in the field coil. This eliminates the risk of overcharging and perhaps destroying the battery. When you over-ride this function, the alternator can pump full charge into the batteries without automatically tapering off as the battery becomes charged.

A variable rheostat can replace this on/off switch, allowing you to increase or decrease the field current and, therefore, the charging rate. But this system requires constant monitoring. You can damage your alternator by overheating it. The chief danger, however, is that you only have to forget just once to switch back to automatic regulation and your batteries will be boiled and permanently damaged. That's a pretty stiff penalty to pay. Even with an automatic shut-off wired in, the variable rheostat is, at best, an old fashioned, partial solution in our quest for more efficient battery charging. There is an optimum charging curve that demands precisely decreasing current at specific battery levels during the charging cycle. Human control, even devoting full attention during the process, is going to be less than perfect.

Today's solution is solid-state electronics and high output alternators with self-governing regulators, such as the series marketed by Balmar Products. These units measure the condition of each battery and automatically regulate charge according to the ideal charging curve, a more efficient and much safer alternative to the old manual control methods.

Mounting a non-standard regulator may require some minor customizing of the engine brackets. It's possible that the increased side load on the fan belt may cause bearings to wear rapidly. Before increasing the size of your alternator, consult the engine manufacturer for approval. When you upgrade your boat's alternator, leave the original unit mounted in place, if possible, to facilitate a temporary switchover if the big one ever fails. Otherwise, clean the old one, spray it thoroughly with light oil, wrap it in plastic, and store it away in a dry locker. It is always wise for a cruising sailboat to carry a spare alternator, as well as replacement brushes and bearings for all alternators you have aboard.

Power Charger

If you need more battery charge than you're getting from the sun, wind, and water generators, there is a diesel-powered alternative to running the engine. Balmar Products markets the Power Charger, comprised of a 4-horsepower Yanmar diesel engine that drives a large (100-amp or 140-amp) Balmar alternator. It is compact, weighs just 65 lbs. and burns only a pint of diesel fuel per hour. For boats with large power consumption devices like DC refrigeration and microwave oven, the Power Charger may be a valuable part of an integrated, ample charging system. From the spare pulley provided, you could drive a mechanical refrigerator compressor at the same time, or a scuba compressor, or auxiliary, large capacity water pump for a deck wash and/or emergency bilge pump. Balmar offers an optional water desalinator that runs off this unit, producing buckets of fresh water while you charge your batteries and fridge.

The WhisperGen, from Victron Energy, represents a new

ıch to generating power and heat on board a yacht. With a weight of only about 41 lbs. and measuring 17.55 x 19.5 x 25.35 inches, the WhisperGen will provide limitless hot water, space heating and battery charging that can be automated. The daily charging capability is 1500 amp-hours with a 12-volt battery bank, or 750 amp-hours with a 24-volt battery bank. What is so special about the WhisperGen, however, is that it is said to go unnoticed: no noise, no vibration, and no fumes. There is a web site describing the product in detail, online at http://www.victronenergie.com/Products/whispergen/whispergen.htm

AC Power Sources

While a 12-volt DC electrical system satisfies most of the needs of most cruising boats, there are certainly occasions when 120-volt AC power is desirable. Operating hand tools such as drills and saber saws, galley appliances such as microwave ovens, blenders, and coffee makers—and on large boats the conveniences of air conditioning, washers, dryers and high-capacity water makers—may be considered important. Here's an overview of several different ways to obtain 120-volt AC power aboard your boat.

Besides shore power, which of course is restricted to dockside use, essentially there are four possibilities: (1) carry a portable gasoline or diesel AC generator or install a heavy duty gen-set; (2) install an inverter to make AC power from your ship's DC batteries; (3) install an engine driven AC generator; (4) install an AC electric generator powered by the ship's DC batteries. A fifth type, seldom if ever seen on boats, is the emergency standby generator system that operates on LPG or LNG. Manufactured by Winco in 5,000- and 8,000-watt models, it is available from the Hamilton Ferris Company.

Before buying an AC power source, make a detailed list of all electrical appliances aboard and the number of watts consumed. Include lights, stereos, TVs, hair dryers, tools, air conditioning and so on. Electric motors (circular saws, air compressors) may require up to five times their normal operating wattage during start-up; this is called surge and must be factored into your calculations. List normal watts and surge watts separately. You probably won't run all appliances at the same time, but the power rating of your AC source (inverter, gen-set, and so on) should exceed by a safe margin the number of watts you expect to use.

Portable Generators and Generators

For many small boat cruisers, fossil-fueled portable generators provide all the intermittent AC required. Numerous manufacturers such as Honda, Yamaha, Tanaka and Nissan sell small, lightweight (20 pounds and up) and inexpensive ($350 and up) generators to the RV market. Yanmar makes a line of portable diesel generators, starting at two kilowatts and 127 pounds. While most are not made of marine-grade materials, commonsense maintenance and weather protection enable them to survive at sea for many years. The units stow handily in cockpit lockers. They are perhaps most useful for powering hand tools and as emergency back-ups for battery charging.

Larger boats with electric stoves, air conditioning and other luxury appliances have little choice but to permanently install a full-sized generator, or gen-set. Because electrical equipment in the United States is designed to operate with a fixed frequency of 60 Hz, the frequency output of the generator must be fixed at 1200, 1800, or 3600 rpm. The slower-turning engines are quieter but heavier than the fast-turning models. The 1800-rpm, four-pole set is a good compromise for many boats.

In most boats the gen-set may be mounted in the engine room. In any case, it must be ventilated, sealed from the living cabins, convenient for fuel and raw-water hook-ups, and mounted on sturdy structural members. Unless you're very knowledgeable about such installations, this is a job best left to professionals. Many of the major manufacturers, including Northern Lights, Onan, Kohler, Westerbeke and Medalist Universal Motors, publish useful manuals to help select, install and maintain their products.

Power Inverters

A power inverter is an electrical device that changes direct current from the ship's batteries into alternating current and boosts voltage from 12 to 120. Unlike some older models, the sophisticated modern inverter, such as the Heart Interface Power Inverter, produces a smooth sine wave suitable for running TVs and computers. It is a good method of obtaining intermittent AC power, but of course it is limited by the capacity of the battery bank; the more ampere-hours in the bank, the longer the inverter can be run. Unlike the generator, it is not a power source, but simply a means of changing electrical current from one form to another. Some principal manufacturers are Balmar, Dytek, Heart, IMI/Kenyon and Trace. Prices range from about $100 (for a small 100-watt model) to $3,500 (for a powerful 2,000-watt model with battery charger). Optional add-ons increase usefulness and cost. A power inverter is a convenient addition to the integrated energy system on a cruising boat. It provides AC electricity without relying on fossil fuels.

Engine-Driven AC Generators

While a gen-set is merely an AC generator directly geared to an internal combustion engine, the engine-driven AC generator just uses the main engine instead of an auxiliary, dedicated one. Engine-driven AC generators such as those made by Auto-Gen mount on or near the main propulsion engine and are driven by belts and pulleys. AC power is available whenever the engine is run. Auto-Gen units are available from 2.5 kilowatts to 6.5 kilowatts and cost from about $2,000 to around $3,000.

AC Electric Generators

Like an inverter, the AC electric generator makes AC from DC, but not by the same means. The AC electric generator uses battery power to run a small electric motor, which then turns the generator. Honeywell is one of several manufacturers; its units produce from 500 to 1,600 watts. Again, such a device is limited by the ampere-hour capacity of the battery bank.

There is no single right product for cruising boats. Just as an integration of two or more 12-volt solar, wind and water generators helps to meet the varying conditions found under way and at anchor, a combination of AC power sources offers versatility. For example, if the genset is operated only when the main engine is shut off, an inverter or engine-driven AC generator can provide AC under way. It really depends on the number and type of appliances installed aboard your boat, and how you use them.

Shore Power

Many cruising sailors spend as little time as possible dockside. Nevertheless, we may at times tie up and plug in, so shore power should figure into our ship's integrated energy system.

For our purposes, the plus-or-minus 120-volt, alternating current brought aboard through the dockside power cable needs to be converted or rectified into direct current at 12 volts. This current can then charge the boat's batteries to supply all our electrical needs while we're plugged in. (Note that in many countries and throughout Europe, a boat that has been wired for American voltage will need a 220/110 step-down voltage transformer to avail itself of shore power.)

For dockside charging, modern boats use a marine AC converter/battery charger. This differs from an ordinary automotive battery charger in two important ways: (1) the design ensures electrical isolation between the 120-volt AC circuit and the battery circuit, which prevents stray currents that pose shock hazards aboard a boat and could set up corrosive electricity in the surrounding water; (2) the converter produces a non-trickle type charge delivery, which avoids the risk of damaging batteries by overcharging. The marine charger automatically shuts itself off when batteries are fully charged, and switches back on when battery voltage drops.

Remember to shut down any alternate energy sources, like solar and wind, that aren't self-regulating. Overcharging batteries is one of the quickest ways to destroy them.

Storage Batteries

Batteries are the heart of the integrated energy system. Because the living environment of a boat requires relatively low amperage doled out over a long period of time, we use *deep cycle* batteries—batteries designed for gradual discharge—to power our lights, radios, and so on. Deep cycle batteries are built more heavily than *starter* batteries, which are designed to deliver lots of amps briefly as for starting an engine.

The first consideration for the battery bank in a successful energy system is its capacity. To some extent, capacity is determined by how much space, weight and money we can afford. Most stock boats do not come with enough battery capacity for liveaboard cruising. Ideally, the ship's batteries should be able to supply nominal electrical energy for four 24-hour days of liveaboard consumption without recharging.

To compute how much energy you typically consume, see the side-bar "Typical Electrical Loads For Accessories". For each item, multiply the amperage it consumes by the number of hours you use that device per day to give you the ampere-hours (amp-hours) drawn. For example, you may burn the anchor light for 11 hours per night. It draws 1.2 amps. So the daily consumption is 13.2 amp-hours (1.2 amps x 11 hours). You might play the stereo for a few hours in the evening: 1 amp x 3 hours = 3 amp-hours. Total up all the amp-hours you've calculated, and you have your approximate daily electrical energy consumption. Consider that your usage is quite different during offshore passages, where running lights, radar, and navigational devices are usually operating for long periods. Depending on your cruising style, you might average this in to your overall average consumption. Now, multiply the total daily amp-hours times four. If your batteries can deliver this total without requiring recharging, you've got an adequate battery bank aboard.

Batteries cannot deliver their rated capacity. To do so would drain them flat, and that's a sure way to shorten the life of a lead-acid battery. It is healthiest for batteries to be recharged once they've reached their 50% capacity. The 50% discharge point of deep cycle, 12-volt batteries is 12.2 volts (we monitor battery voltage from an accurate voltmeter). But even 50% is too much to expect, because our batteries are not always charged to capacity. In fact, after normal charging, they're

Typical Electrical Loads For Accessories
Estimated power consumption
of some common on board devices

Device	Amps*	Device	Amps*
Anchor Light	1.2	Loran	1.2
Anchor Windlass	75.0	Masthead Tri-color	2.0
Autopilot	4.0	Microwave (via inverter)	95.0
Bilge Blower	2.5	Propane Electric Shut-Off	0.7
Bilge Pump	4.0	Radar	3.7
Cabin Fan	1.2	Recording Depthsounder	0.5
Cabin Light (incandescent)	1.5	Refrigeration (cycling)	25.0
CB Radio (receive)	1.0	Running Lights	3.5
Compass Light	0.1	Sat Nav (average)	0.3
Deck Wash Pump	10.0	Spreader Lights	6.0
Depth Sounder	0.1	Spotlight	10.0
Fluorescent Light	0.5	Steaming Light	1.0
Forced Air Heater	7.0	SSB Radio (receive)	2.0
Foredeck Light	1.7	SSB Radio (transmit)	25.0
Fresh Water Pump	8.0	Strobe Light	0.7
Fuel Pump	3.0	Tape Player	1.0
GPS	1.5	VHF Radio (receive)	0.3
Head Pump	18.0	VHF Radio (transmit)	4.5
Horn	3.0	Watermaker (small 12-volt)	3.6
Inverter	1.4	Weather Fax	2.4
Knot Meter	0.1	Wind Speed Indicator	0.1

* To estimate the amperage draw of other 12-volt devices, divide their rated watts by 12.

only at about 85%. So, in order to limit discharge to the 50% level, we have just 35% of the rated capacity of our bank available for use without recharging (85% charged–50% discharge level = 35% available).

This means we want our 4-day amp-hours to equal 35% or less of our batteries' rated capacity. Let's assume a 50 amp-hour daily usage aboard. That's 200 amp-hours for four days. This indicates a battery bank rated for about 572 amp-hours (35% of 572 = 200.2), requiring three or four large, deep cycle batteries.

Do yourself a great favor and invest in top quality batteries. Their price may be higher at purchase, but their cost will ultimately be lower when averaged out over years of continued use beyond the life span of cheaper brands, not to mention the reliability factor.

Batteries are best mounted low in the boat because they're so heavy and can affect boat stability and trim. However, they must also sit above high bilge-water levels. The less distance between energy sources, batteries, and loads (distribution panel and appliances), the better, because power is lost in long wire runs. Batteries shouldn't be allowed to get very hot, as they will if installed in most engine compartments. Heating will shorten their life considerably. They need to be secured so that they can't possibly come loose, even if the boat is turned upside down and shaken. If they're lead-acid batteries, they need to be in strong battery boxes that will catch any acid that leaks, and they should be ventilated. Be sure the installation is readily accessible for routine maintenance.

You have the option of using pairs of 6-volt batteries, connected in series, instead of single 12-volt batteries. These may be easier to move around and install. There's the added advantage that if one cell goes bad, ruining the battery, you only have to replace half as much battery.

Battery technology continues to evolve. Lead-acid batteries are probably still the most commonly seen 12-volt battery type, but in the 1980s, gel packed batteries became available and offered several advantages over lead-acid batteries: Gel batteries cannot spill acid, they don't form dangerous gases while charging, they're totally maintenance-free (never needing water added), and, according to most manufacturers, they can be discharged flat without harm. The only way to damage gel batteries is by overheating or overcharging them. In size, weight, price, and longevity they're comparable to top quality lead-acid batteries.

Today, AGM (Absorption Glass Mat) batteries represent the next step in both deep cycle and starter battery technology. AGM sealed batteries were originally developed in the early 1980s for military aircraft where power, weight, safety, and reliability were important considerations. They're ideal for marine, RV, and aviation applications, claiming increased safety, performance, and service life over other existing sealed battery types, including gel technology. AGM batteries deliver and absorb higher rates of amperage during discharging and charging. In addition, they can be charged at normal lead-acid regulated charging voltages, so it's not necessary to recalibrate charging systems or purchase special chargers.

Distribution

If the batteries are the heart of the integrated energy system, then the distribution system is the brain. Distribution of electricity aboard happens in two stages: First, source energy is consigned to one or more of the batteries. Then the stored energy in the batteries is directed to each device as needed.

Source energy other than that of the alternator (i.e., current from solar panels, wind and water generators, battery chargers) may be channeled through switches enabling us to manually determine the target battery, the battery that receives that charge (see Figure 20). Or, each of these trickle charges can simply be wired directly to one specific battery. If, for example, we have dedicated one battery to power a 12-volt refrigerator compressor, usually the heaviest load aboard, we can expect this battery to be depleted daily. It's going to need almost constant replenishment of energy. If the wind generator is the most consistent producer aboard, we can wire it to this refrigerator battery (we'll call it battery #1). In breezy conditions such as the tradewinds, a full-size wind generator can generate 100 amp-hours or more daily, enough to keep battery #1 topped off.

Now, suppose the wind is up and the wind generator is cranking out a steady 9 amps—over 200 amp hours in 24 hours. That's more than the refrigerator battery can use. We'll want to share some of those spare amps with other batteries. We could use some to top off the reserve or starter battery (#2) if we've dedicated one, or to supplement the house bank (#3). This sharing is accomplished through a pair of master battery selector switches, through which we can connect #1 with #2, or #1 with #3, or #2 with #3 (see Figure 20—Wiring Diagram). Electricity will flow from whichever bank has the higher voltage to the bank that has the lower voltage. Like water, voltage seeks its own level. Therefore, soon after two batteries are connected through the switch, they'll level off at the mean voltage. In our example we'll connect the wind-charged refrigerator battery (#1) to the house bank (#3). First they'll level off. Then, as more of the wind generator's trickle charge enters battery #1, half of it will bleed over to #3, keeping them both charged to the same level.

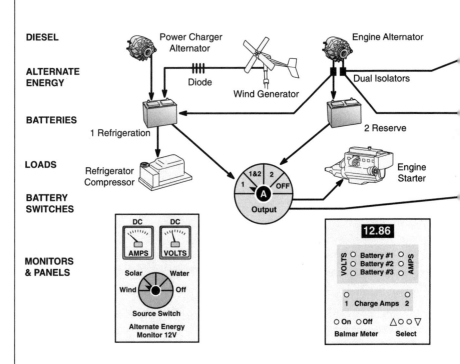

From top left: A Power Charger will guarantee ample, efficient recharging for the #1 (refrigerator) battery and, through the switches, the #2 and #3 banks as well. The wind generator also feeds directly to Battery #1.

The main engine's large alternator charges all battery banks, each according to need, distributed by a pair of dual isolators.

Battery #2 is a reserve battery. It sometimes functions as an engine starter battery, and sometimes as a second refrigerator battery, as determined by the switch positions.

Solar and water generators feed the #3 (house) battery bank. This house bank, which is shown as a pair of 12-volt batteries in parallel, also receives the battery charger's input when shore power is available. When shore power is disconnected, the power inverter can supply 120-volt AC to the ship's electrical sockets, drawing 12-volt current from the #3 bank.

The #4 battery is dedicated to an electric anchor windlass. It is mounted far from the rest of the system, requiring long wire runs. For this reason, and since it normally is used with the engine running, the Battery #4 is only charged by the engine alternator and cannot interact with the other banks through the switches, as can Batteries #1, #2, and #3.

The Switches: The system requires two four-position battery switches. Switch A receives Batteries #1 and #2. The output of this switch is used for engine starting. If Switch A is pointing to #1, then that battery will be called upon to start the engine (#1 is already feeding the refrigerator directly). The 1 & 2 setting combines these two batteries in parallel, for boosting the refrigerator battery's capacity, or for engine starting with two batteries. Set to #2 alone, it uses the reserve battery for starting.

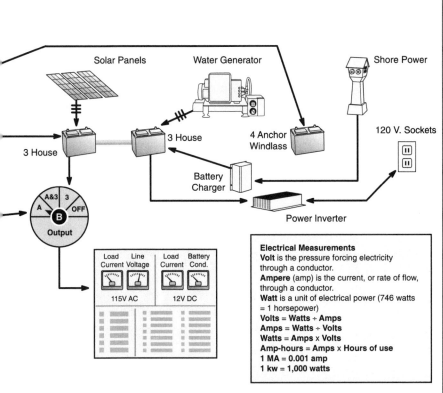

Electrical Measurements
Volt is the pressure forcing electricity through a conductor.
Ampere (amp) is the current, or rate of flow, through a conductor.
Watt is a unit of electrical power (746 watts = 1 horsepower)
Volts = Watts ÷ Amps
Amps = Watts ÷ Volts
Watts = Amps x Volts
Amp-hours = Amps x Hours of use
1 MA = 0.001 amp
1 kw = 1,000 watts

The output of Switch A also goes to the A-terminal on Switch B. Switch B is also wired to the #3 battery bank. In the middle (A&3) position, Switch B connects the #3 bank with whatever Switch A is set to. So, if Switch A is set on #1, and Switch B is set on A & 3, then battery banks #1 and #3 are connected. This would be a useful setting when shore power is connected, enabling the charge to flow into #3, then onward into #1 to keep the refrigerator battery topped off as well as the house bank. Output of Switch B goes to the distribution panel.

Monitors: The alternate energy monitor illustrated uses one pair of meters—a DC amps meter and a DC volts meter—to monitor three alternate energy sources. The meters display the output of whichever source the four-position switch is set to: wind generator, solar panels or water generator.

The Balmar digital meter displays the precise voltage of any one of three battery banks. It also displays the number of amperes flowing into or out of each battery, and how many amps are being produced by either of two sources (one source normally being the engine's alternator).

The distribution panel shown also houses four meters:
120-volt AC Load Current—how many amps of AC we are consuming
120-volt AC Line Voltage—how much AC voltage is being supplied
12-volt DC Load Current—the total DC amps we're using
12-volt DC Battery Condition—approximate battery voltage level

Courtesy of Cruising World

Conversely, when the refrigerator compressor cycles on while #1 and #3 are connected, it will be drawing from both batteries simultaneously. There are times when this may be desirable and times when it is not. The main thing is that we are in control.

The one energy source that ought to be automatic is the alternator. This can and should be self-distributing as well as self-regulating. By wiring the alternator through isolators, its charge is directed to all batteries. A dual isolator enables you to charge 2 separate battery banks simultaneously. A pair of dual isolators charges 4 banks, regardless of the battery selector switch positions. The isolators determine which batteries need how much of the charge, and distribute the alternator's amperage output accordingly. So if the house bank is low when you fire up the engine, but the refrigerator battery is well charged from alternate sources, then the alternator will jam maximum amps into the hungry #3 battery, while sending only a trickle to #1. Finally, as all batteries approach a charged condition, the self-regulating alternator gradually reduces its output to zero.

Once energy is directed to and stored in the batteries, it can then travel to the ship's electrical panel, stage two of the distribution system. The modern panel includes rows of breaker switches, each one labeled for its load device. Panels can be placed in almost any convenient area away from possible spray from hatches, the nearer to the batteries, the better. (*Warning:* Many panels have AC and DC on the same board, albeit in separate rows. If you're ever poking around behind such a panel while plugged into shore power, and accidentally cross an AC terminal with a DC terminal with your screwdriver, a massive dose of electricity may be instantly distributed into you, or, through the negative grounded engine, into the surrounding water. Someone could get electrocuted. All 120-volt AC breaker panels should be physically separated from 12-volt DC panels. They rarely are, so be careful.)

From the panel, myriad wires run throughout the boat to the appliances. They should be color coded and recorded in diagram form for future reference. Neat, tie-wrapped bundles of wire, well secured to bulkheads along their route, are the mark of a professional installation. Most devices call for an in-line fuse of proper amperage, a smart precaution even if the panel's breakers perform the same protective function.

In general, unless you're especially well versed in wiring, you should hire, or at least consult, a professional marine electrician regarding wire sizes, insulation, connections, diodes, fuses, switches, and safety precautions. Faulty or improper wiring is a prime cause of fires on boats.

Monitor and Control

The monitors are the eyes of the integrated energy system. By observing how much current passes in and out of the system, and how much we have stored, we can more effectively control and conserve electricity aboard. We can also protect the system from damage due to negligence.

Monitors, for our purposes, are meters. There are two basic types we can use: analog models; and the newer, extremely accurate, solid-state digital meters with LCD readouts. The latter are the better choice where accuracy is desired, such as observing battery voltage.

Monitoring the incoming source energy can be accomplished with simple analog meters. One AC voltmeter can display shore power when we're plugged in dockside and an AC ammeter will indicate how much of a load we're putting on the AC system. This will help us avoid overloading the 30-amp or 50-amp circuits that moderate-size sailboats commonly use. Away from the dock, the same AC meters will indicate voltage provided by, and amps drawn from the power inverter or gen-set, if they're used.

We want to know how much energy our alternate sources are providing. DC volt meters, wired to the solar, wind, and water generators, illustrate at what point these units are developing enough voltage to start pumping amps into the batteries. Even more useful are DC ammeters. Wired to the source generators, they register how many amps each unit is producing. Knowing this, we can easily judge whether these sources are keeping pace with our consumption, and which ones are helping the most at what times. A single voltmeter and a single amp meter can serve to monitor all three alternate energy sources, one at a time, if you wire in a three-way switch to each meter.

Similarly, one analog voltage meter can monitor all the batteries if a switch is wired in line to connect the meter with each battery separately, one at a time. An off position in the switch will conserve power, avoid-ing the inevitable small draw of a meter in constant operation. One DC ammeter should monitor the total amperage consumption aboard.

Watch the batteries closely. Neglecting them will surely result in damage. We need to know when our batteries reach the 50% dis-charge point (12.2 volts) to avoid deep-cycle discharge, which short-ens battery life. Conversely, we must guard against overcharging that can ruin a battery.

The old fashioned way to determine lead-acid battery condition is by measuring the specific gravity of the sulfuric acid and water elec-trolyte with a hydrometer, a glass tube with a calibrated float inside and a rubber suction bulb on top. This is still a good gauge for identifying a bad cell, but the measurement is affected by temperature variations, making it a less than perfect means of determining voltage. Besides, it's a hassle to use as often as we'll want that information. An accurate voltmeter is what's needed. In the analog category, an *expanded-scale suppressed-zero* analog meter is the best choice. It ignores voltages below 10 or 11, because a battery is completely dead and depleted of useful charge at that point anyway. Instead, this meter's scale makes it easier to read exact fractions of volts by only displaying levels between, say, 10 and 16.

The most accurate meters are the digital models. A multi-function digital meter can display the voltage level of three separate batteries (measured to the 100th of a volt), and the amperage passing in and out of each. It also monitors the amperage output of two or more energy sources, one normally being the alternator. Selector buttons let us choose what information is displayed on the LCD screen. With this monitor system, it's easy to check the voltage of each battery with a glance, several times daily. We can also see instantly whether a battery is gaining or losing amps, as loads that are consuming power compete with sources putting energy back in.

As you get used to making quick, regular surveys of your ship's energy components, you will find your confidence increasing with your ability to monitor and control your integrated energy system. For the cruising sailor, an intelligent, ample and robust electrical system is a key to better living afloat.

Chapter 14

⌒⌒

Mechanical Considerations

The Engine

All but the most devout purist and the most budget-restrained will want an auxiliary engine in their cruising sailboat. In my early cruising days, I fitted into both categories and sailed an old gaff-rigged ketch sans engine for a few years. I learned a lot of boat handling under sail only, and I still make a point of anchoring and docking boats that way, at least often enough to remember how. The one thing about an engine that you can count on is that it will eventually break down, so you ought to be able to maneuver your boat safely into port using sail power alone. Practice makes perfect.

Once you're in port with an ailing engine, you'll need good access to facilitate repair work. If your boat doesn't provide for this adequately, see what you can do about improving the situation. Sometimes cutting doorways or hatches in the side or top of the engine compartment will enable you to reach otherwise difficult areas. For example, in some boats a removable panel in the quarter berth may permit you to quickly reach the stuffing box and transmission area, and the fuel filters. For major overhauls, the cockpit sole on some boats is, or can be made, removable by unbolting. Then the engine can be more easily removed should that become necessary. Engine accessibility and removability are important considerations for the cruising sailor, so review your boat's arrangement with an eye for possible ways to improve it.

How big an engine is big enough? Some old-timers say if it will push the boat at hull speed in calm conditions, it's the right size. I think that's a bit light for the modern cruiser. Three and a half to four horsepower for every ton of displacement seems like a reasonable average for a mid-sized cruising sailboat. Because of the risk of explosion from gasoline vapors, diesel engines are definitely preferable. Only on a small pocket cruiser would I consider using an outboard motor as the auxiliary engine.

How much fuel capacity is enough? The more the better, I suppose. SPARROW's fuel tank was only 40 U.S. gallons, but when heading offshore I carried an additional 17 gallons in 3 jerrycans. Averaging 5 1/2 knots offshore, SPARROW's fuel consumption rate was about 0.5 gallons per hour (0.65 gph if I speed up to 6 1/2 knots). So my 57 gallons of fuel could yield about a 600 nautical mile motoring range—a bit more if I conserved; a bit less if I rushed it. There are times I would have liked having twice that range, but SPARROW and I managed to get around all right with what we had, including two Atlantic crossings.

To prevent seawater from entering the engine block in following seas, the exhaust must have an effective anti-siphon loop, a water lift muffler system, and a thru-hull shut off valve. Also note that, if your engine compartment is ever flooded, a diesel engine can continue running as long as the air intake remains above the water level. I've seen installations that include a vertical air intake extension pipe that reaches nearly to the top of the engine compartment. With this, the engine can operate even if it's otherwise completely submerged.

I am not a mechanic; more like what they call a "wrench." But I can read the engine manual, figure out how to do most things myself, and religiously follow the prescribed maintenance schedule. This includes regular changes of oil and filters. It's worthwhile to set up an easy system for changing the oil by installing a manual or electric oil sump pump, or a petcock drain installed in the lowest section of the engine oil pan if access to it is possible. These can make draining out the old oil a snap. Assign a jug to contain waste oil until it can be properly disposed of ashore. The easier you make oil changes, the less likely you are to procrastinate.

I make a point of wiping the engine and its surroundings clean with a household cleaner and a rag, at least monthly and after every oil change. This makes it a more pleasant place to work, and it is easier to spot any leaks or rusting.

Fuel Filters

In addition to the engine's own fuel filter, install at least one in-line water separator/fuel filter. Better yet, install two. They can save your engine. I once bought a tank-full of contaminated diesel from a very respectable looking American fuel dock. Soon after, the engine stalled. The fuel supply had been completely choked by sludge and water, contaminants that were in the fuel I bought, which accumulated in the Racor fuel filter/water separator. However, none of the debris reached the engine. The filter prevented the filth from entering the injectors and so prevented serious damage. Because I had two fuel filters installed in line, I simply switched over to the fresh filter and cleaned the polluted one while underway.

At least one mechanic I know claims that the most common fuel filter problem is caused by cheap fuel additives containing alcohol. They can break down the plastic and rubber parts in the filters. Use a diesel fuel additive to protect the system against fungus, but select your brand carefully. Read the ingredients to be certain it does not contain alcohol.

Seawater Strainer

The seawater that cools the engine must be filtered or *strained* before it reaches the water pump. Straining catches seaweed, grass, mud, plastic, and other debris, trapping them in a screen mesh before they can get into and harm the engine's cooling system. Groco Marine manufactures a sturdy unit in a clear glass and cast bronze case, making it easy to check and clean the screening cylinder inside. The strainer is mounted to any convenient bulkhead, in-line between the raw water intake thru-hull fitting and the engine. Additionally, a small bronze or stainless steel grille mounted over the thru-hull on the outside of the hull is the first line of defense, preventing most bigger debris from ever entering the system at all. These grilles are available at marine chandleries and must be installed while the boat is hauled out or careened.

Automatic Fire Extinguishing System

Consider installing a heat-triggered engine compartment fire extinguisher, a safety feature that may do more than improve your insurance rate. A small unit usually suffices in a sailboat (consult the manufacturer for the correct size to use). Install an indicator light to notify you if the automatic system has been activated, and some means of manually activating the system from outside the engine compartment.

Gauges and Alarms

It is reckless to cruise without engine gauges that display oil pressure and water temperature. Check them often when the engine is running. An engine hour meter is also a very good idea so that you can schedule timely maintenance routines.

A cruising boat is no place for the idiot lights, the little red indicator lights on the panel that come on when something's wrong. Even with proper gauges, it isn't possible for the captain and crew to constantly monitor every system. So consider installing alarms to warn you of dangerous situations such as low engine oil pressure, high engine temperature, high water levels in the bilge, propane accumulation in the bilge, smoke in the engine compartment and the saloon, and discharge of the automatic fire extinguisher system. You could hook up all these alarms to a single sound device, with individually labeled indicator lights and on/off switches. Alarms are cheap insurance and can pay for themselves a thousand-fold the first time one of them provides an early warning of a developing problem.

Engine Controls

I prefer a single lever engine control rather than separate levers for throttle and gearshift. The single lever leaves one hand free to steer when shifting between forward and reverse, as during docking maneuvers. Boats with wheel pedestals normally have these controls mounted on the pedestal. On a boat with tiller steering, mounting a single lever control low on the cockpit's side permits operation with one foot.

Propellers

The first choice to make regarding your boat's propeller is between a two-bladed and a three-bladed prop. The fixed two-bladed propeller creates less drag when sailing if it is locked in a vertical position. However, it is a bit less efficient in forward gear and considerably less effective in reverse than a propeller with three blades. On the other hand, the more powerful three-bladed prop presents more surface area to passing water when the boat is sailing and thus produces more drag, slowing the boat a bit when sailing.

Folding propellers minimize drag while sailing. The blades collapse around the hub when not being spun. However, this prop is reportedly very hard on certain transmissions. Consult your engine and transmission manufacturer. If you do switch your boat's original propeller for another, more efficient model, keep the old one aboard as a spare.

There's another alternative, which provides the best of these various characteristics: a three-blade feathering propeller (see Figures 21a and 21b), such as the popular Max-Prop. A feathering propeller significantly reduces underwater drag while sailing. This is because on a feathering prop, the blades pivot to present their edge to the passing water when the engine is not spinning the prop. So the propeller trails with minimal drag. Try dragging an oar alongside a moving boat sometime, first with the flat side facing the water flow, then turned 90 degrees so the thin edge is forward. This will give you an exaggerated idea of the reduced drag a feathering propeller accomplishes when in the neutral

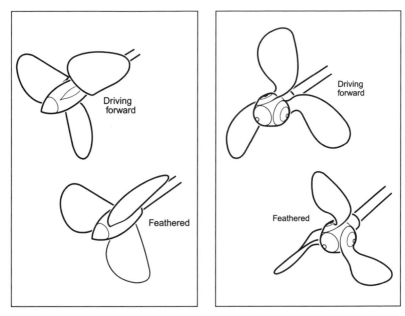

Figures 21a and 21b: The Max-Prop and the Autoprop are two popular feathering propellers. Both pivot their blades edge-on to the flow of water when not being spun by the shaft.

mode for sailing. Many users report a good half-knot increase in sailing speed, which can add up to many miles on a long passage. In addition, it greatly increases the reversing power of the engine because the blades pivot to face aft when spun in reverse. The Max-Prop is superbly machined in Italy and sold for an impressive price in the United States by PYI, Inc. Luke also manufactures a feathering propeller.

The newest evolution of this concept is the Autoprop, advertised as "the world's first self-pitching propeller." Manufactured by Brunton's Propellers and distributed in the United States by Autoprop in Newport, Rhode Island, these smart props were first introduced to the European market in 1987, and have more recently earned growing acceptance in the U.S. and elsewhere. The Autoprop reportedly develops more thrust at any given engine speed, ahead or astern, than fixed, folding, or feathering propellers. Like the Max-Prop, the Autoprop's three blades align themselves with the flow of the water when you're

sailing with the shaft restrained from turning, and so r
up to 85%.

What makes the Autoprop unique is its ability to _____
vary the propeller pitch according to the vessel's speed and the resist-
ance it is encountering. The manufacturer asserts that when a vessel is
motor sailing, the Autoprop adopts a coarse pitch setting by taking into
account the driving force of the sails. This results in increased speed at
very low engine revolutions. By constantly operating at the optimum
pitch setting, better speeds are achieved and range is increased. The
blades automatically optimize pitch to allow more revs to be developed
in adverse conditions. In reverse gear, the blades' leading edges are the
same as in forward, unlike a fixed propeller, so backing down is more
controlled. An Autoprop will probably fit your existing shaft and is
compatible with all makes of rope cutters.

For optimum maneuvering control on sailboats over, say, 50 feet,
a bow thruster may be worth having. Installed below the waterline
in a tube at the bow and triggered by a toggle switch at the helm station, a bow thruster pushes the bow of a boat to port or starboard by
means of a powerful electric propeller. It can make docking much easier in difficult conditions. Installation requires cutting a hole right
through the hull to install the tube containing the thruster, a job best
done by professionals.

A less expensive and less intrusive variation of a bow thruster is a
water jet thruster. Jet nozzles are installed in the bow below the waterline, one facing to port and one to starboard. A powerful water pump
forces seawater through the nozzles to push the vessel's bow in the desired direction. From what I've seen and heard, water jet thrusters on
yachts tend to be less powerful than propeller bow thrusters, but it's
possible that increased water pump and nozzle size, combined with
prudent expectations, might make this a smart choice for some boats.

Zincs

Sacrificial zinc anodes are necessary to protect a bronze propeller from
deterioration by electrolysis. Some props are made to take a cap zinc

that fits over the shaft's aft end. In any case, a shaft zinc should be installed on the shaft itself. A small block of zinc bolted onto a metal skeg shoe, or onto the rudder, may further increase the anode protection in that crucial area. I often buy slabs of zinc and cut and drill pieces to fit various applications. You can melt zinc to mold your own specially fitted pieces, too. Carry plenty of spare zinc, and don't be negligent about replacing old, worn pieces. Stock up in advance with any specially made zinc anodes for propeller caps, etc. Zincs are much cheaper to replace than propellers.

Note: If you use a Max-Prop, carry half a dozen spares of the cap zinc bolts. These special bolts tend to get loose and fall out as the zinc deteriorates. You'll be glad to have replacements with you.

In addition to fixed zincs, consider using a *fish* zinc whenever you're in port. I use a 6" x 12" plate of 1/2" zinc, through which I have drilled two holes. One hole is for a piece of line to hang the zinc overboard from the ship's rail, lowered as close to the propeller as possible when at anchor or docked. Through the other hole I fasten one stripped end of a long, sheathed, copper wire. This wire runs inboard, typically through a small, watertight deck fitting, and is connected to the engine's negative grounding plate, the place on the engine block where other negative wires have been attached. By grounding to the engine (and therefore, through the engine to the prop shaft and the propeller), I have made the zinc a sacrificial anode in the electrolytic process that inevitably occurs in salt water. The zinc dissolves instead of the bronze propeller. Manufactured fish zincs can be purchased already made up with the wire attached, sometimes molded in the shape of a fish (what'll they think of next?). A fish zinc is not a replacement for the mounted zincs mentioned above; it's only an added precaution intended to take some of the load off the mounted zincs while in port. Remember to take in your fish zinc before getting under way. Otherwise, it may be sucked into the propeller and damage the blades.

Most engines benefit by having an anode, called a pencil zinc, somewhere in the salt water cooling system to protect internal parts. Find out where it goes in your engine and replace it periodically. If the engine doesn't have one, ask the manufacturer if there's any reason why you shouldn't install one. Consider doing the same for any seawater-cooled systems, such as refrigeration and air conditioning; anywhere salt water contacts dissimilar metals.

Shaft Locking

You'll want some means of preventing the prop shaft from spinning freely while the boat is sailing. Freewheeling—allowing the propeller to spin its shaft while sailing—can harm some transmissions. Even if it doesn't harm your particular transmission, it does create unnecessary wear on the cutless bearing and shaft during long passages, and usually makes a distracting whirring noise. Many engines will lock the prop shaft simply by putting the transmission in forward or reverse gear when the engine is turned off. If your engine's transmission doesn't do this, there are at least two devices available commercially, Prop Lock and Shaft Lok, that do the job. Shaft locking isn't generally necessary with feathering or folding propellers, although in my experience the Max-Prop occasionally needs the shaft stopped for a moment for the passing water to feather the blades while sailing.

Buckets and Bilge Pumps

They say the best bilge pump in the world is a frightened sailor standing knee deep in water with a bucket in his hands. In fact, a bucket is an excellent way to remove copious amounts of water quickly. You should have at least two strong ones available for general use as well as for bailing.

I find that the handles inevitably break off the average store bought bucket, so I replace them straight away with a rope handle. The white plastic commercial food container buckets you find thrown out behind restaurants make excellent, strong, jumbo buckets for a boat. Drill two holes in opposite sides of the bucket's rim, reeve the ends of a 3-foot piece of line through and secure it with stop knots. Presto, instant bucket with a rope handle. Make a small loop in the handle's center for attaching a 6-foot tether and tie a loop or stop knot at the tether's other end for gripping while fetching seawater over the side.

In addition to buckets, you need at least two, preferably three or four, bilge pumps. The basic set includes one electric, high capacity pump with an automatic float switch. The float switch turns on the pump when the bilge's water level rises beyond a certain height and a warning light at the breaker panel indicates that this is happening. You can also install a counter that records the number of times the pump has cycled on during your absence, so you'll know if there's a persistent leak.

Also necessary is at least one manual pump operated from the cockpit. Oversized is the keyword here. Then, if you're prudent, you will repeat the system: a second electric pump in another part of the bilge, and another manual pump, this one operated from belowdecks. The belowdecks manual pump must be installed to discharge water without having to open the cockpit hatch boards, etc. Manual bilge pump handles should be tied to the boat.

In addition, a large capacity, portable hand bilge pump, mounted on a board, can be stored in a locker and then carried to wherever it's needed, including someone else's endangered boat or a swamped dinghy. I've used such a pump several times to help out distressed neighbors.

Bilge pump hoses should loop high above the waterline before exiting at a thru-hull fitting slightly above waterline. Be sure there is an anti-siphon valve installed at the crest of this anti-siphon loop, particularly in the electric pump discharge hose. Otherwise, when the boat is heeled over and the hose's thru-hull fitting is under water, a vacuum may develop and seawater can be sucked into the bilge. This once happened aboard a vessel I was delivering, way offshore late at night in rough seas ("Uh, excuse me, Captain, but the floor boards are floating!") and it took a long, anxious search before I figured out where all that water was entering the boat. To increase your safety factor, you might add a one-way check valve in-line in the hose.

You can install a high capacity bilge pump that is belt-driven off the engine, with a mechanical clutch. If you have installed the engine air intake raised extension pipe I mentioned earlier, this emergency bilge pump could continuously remove large quantities of water for a long time, even with the vessel nearly filled. A simpler, though less effective auxiliary bilge pumping set up calls for an in-line Y-valve that switches the engine's raw water intake from outside seawater to a bilge hose. Be sure the intake is well screened to prevent debris from getting into the cooling system.

Clogging of the intake hose is a common problem with bilge pumps. Several preventive measures are called for: First, keep your bilges sparkling clean, always. The first time you scrub and paint or gelcoat your boat's bilges may be a real chore if you're making up for previous neglect. But after that it's an easy routine to keep them spotless. Second, wrap bronze or plastic screening loosely around all bilge intake hose ends, hose-clamped in place, to form a sphere or cylinder of screened area that extends about 6" beyond the hose's end. This will keep debris out of the hose, but may need occasional cleaning. Finally, don't store paper products, including cans with paper labels, in the bilge areas. Paper of any kind stored in the bilge will inevitably find its way into the bilge pump hoses, clogging them just when you most need them to work.

Chapter 15

⌒⌒

Tools, Chemicals, and Spares

There is no end to what the self-sufficient cruising sailor must repair, replace, maintain, and fabricate. It's amazing what you can learn and do when you have to. For me, this is part of the adventure and appeal of the cruising lifestyle. My abilities and resourcefulness are constantly being challenged and improved. Skills gradually develop to include at least a working knowledge of mechanics, electricity, carpentry, rigging, marlinespike, metalwork, plumbing, and general handywork. The ship's library should include how-to books on all these topics and more.

The right tool for the job is an axiom you'll come to appreciate. Also needed are the right chemicals and the right spare parts. In the course of outfitting the modern cruising sailboat, with all of its complex equipment and systems, we want to be especially conscientious about stocking the necessary tools, chemicals and spares.

The Tool Kit

You will want to carry all the necessary tools. The following list is extensive; it may not be possible to store so many heavy tools on a small boat, so use your own best judgment in deciding what's necessary. Invest in top quality tools and preserve them by periodically coating them with light oil. They'll repay you over the years with reliability and longevity.

Manuals

Carry operation, service and repair manuals, as well as parts catalogs, for every mechanical device and piece of complex equipment aboard. Eventually you'll need them all. In many small ports, skilled repairmen can be found to assist you in making repairs if you just have these manuals and the spare parts they need.

Basic Rigging Tools

- Bosun's chair and pouch with safety harness or lanyard
- Rigging knife
- Sheathed knife kept sharp and handy in cockpit
- Nicopress sleeves for all wire sizes on board
- Bolt-up type swaging tool to press Nicopress sleeves
- Cable cutters
- Diamond rods for hacksaw holder

Basic Sailmaking Tools

- Sail needles, assorted, from size numbers 12 to 19
- Knife
- Side cutters
- Rope fid
- Sailor's palms
- Scissors

- Awl

- Thread and twine

- Nylon or tarred marlin for serving

- Spare Dacron cloth

- Beeswax

- 3/8-inch grommet punch, spare grommets, and dies

- Contact cement for emergency repairs

- Butane pipe lighter to seal line ends

Additional Sailmaking Tools

- Electric portable zigzag sewing machine with hand cranking attachment

- Dies for brass cringle liners

- Soft hammer

- Seam ripper

- 12-volt and 110-volt soldering guns with flat tip for hot knifing Dacron cloth

- Rigging vise and wire fids

- Various weights of spare cloth and bolt rope materials

- 100-foot measuring tape

- Nylon webbing and tape

- Rip-Stop sail tape

- Leather

- Scraps of colored nylon for making flags

Basic Carpentry Tools

- Wood chisels (1/4", 1/2", and 1")
- Smoothing plane
- Surform planes
- Back saw, hand saw
- Claw hammer
- Counterbores for wood screws
- Brace and bits 1/4" to 1-inch and expandable to 1 1/2"
- Egg beater drill
- Four or five adjustable clamps or C-clamps, various sizes
- Two speed hand drill plus set of bits including many small size bits that break easily
- 12-foot tape measure
- Paint and varnish brushes
- Oil can
- Putty knife
- Caulking gun and cartridges
- Wood scraper and fine file
- Wood rasp (file)
- Box of assorted sand paper, various grits (regular, wet/dry, and emery paper)
- 8"x 12" carpenter's square
- Bevel gauge, marking gauge
- Whetstones, large and small

Additional Carpentry Tools (for wooden boat or professional use)

- 6-foot folding rule

- Set of hole saws

- Draw knife

- Caulking tools including making iron, nib iron, reefing irons

- Caulking mallet

- Wood plug cutters of 3/8", 1/2", and 5/8" to fit your counter bores

- Screwdriver bits for brace

- Additional chisels and planes

- Coping saw, dovetail saw

- Angle grinder

- Scribe

- Spoke shave

- Additional wood scrapers

Basic Mechanic's Tools

- Several sizes of adjustable crescent wrenches

- Assorted screwdrivers

- Phillips screwdrivers

- Vise grips, several sizes

- Pliers

- Needle-nose pliers

- Channel lock pliers

- Cold chisel, various sizes
- Fine flat file, coarse half round bastard, various round files
- High speed drill bits, 1/16" to 1/2", 3/8" shanks
- 2 hacksaws and 12 assorted spare blades
- Small pipe wrench
- Ball peen hammer
- 3/8" or 1/2" drive socket set
- Combination wrenches up to 1"
- Feeler gauge
- Nut drivers
- Allen (hex) wrenches
- Water pump pliers
- Tap and die set
- Machinist square and straight edge
- Inside/outside calipers
- 8" and 14" pipe wrenches
- Valve grinding compound
- Countersinks
- Center punches
- Side cutters
- Pin punches
- Selection of brass rod for soft punches 1/4" to 3/4" x 6"
- Stainless steel bristle wire brushes

- Pry bar

- Tin snips

Additional Mechanic's Tools

- Small and large assorted metal files and cold chisels

- Chain wrench

- 3-foot pipe to fit over wrench handles for leverage

- Impact driver

- Micrometers

- Various gear pullers

- Torque wrench

- Large set of Allen wrenches

- Set of easy-outs

- Service wrenches for A/C and refrigeration valves

- Re-Coil (or Heil-a-Coil) kits, 1/4 x 20 and 3/8 x 16

Basic Electrician's Tools

- Hydrometer (battery tester)

- Electrical tape

- Multi-tester volt/ohm/amp meter

- Soldering iron with various size tips, solder (solid, resin, and acid core), and soldering paste (flux)

- Butane soldering torch

- Wire stripper

- Terminal crimper

- Selection of connectors and crimp ends

- Side cutters

- Electrical contact cleaner

- Wire of various colors and sizes

- Variety of quick-ties and wire bundle clamps

- Assortment of heat-shrink tubing

- Small vise

- Pigtail. A short length of cable with one end that plugs into and extends your shore power cord, and the other end left unfinished to accept various cable ends used in foreign marinas. With this, you can make up your own adapter with just one local fitting to install.

Electric Power Tools

- 3" belt sander with assorted spare belts

- 3/8" drill with bits

- Grinder/sander, with discs and soft pad

- Vibrator sander

- Circular saw with assorted blades and abrasive cutting discs

- Saber saw with assorted blades

- Step-up/step-down converter for 220 volt to 110 volt so power tools can be used in other countries

- Heavy-duty extension cords including at least one long enough to reach the masthead. Also, a couple of household extension cords for light applications.

Plumbing Tools

- 3 sizes Stillson wrenches

- Tubing tools for cutting and flaring

- Monkey wrench

Miscellaneous Tools

- Freon leak detector (for refrigeration and air conditioning)

- Refrigeration pressure gauge

- Chain binder (load binder)

- Crow bar

- 5-lb. sledge hammer

- Single bit hatchet or axe

- Short-handled shovel

- Machete

- Small, flat hydraulic jack

- Ratchet hoist (come-along), 3-ton capacity

- Propeller puller

- Magnet, 5-lb. capacity

- Small magnet on a stick to retrieve tools and parts

- Small mirror on a stick

- Long garden hose with spare end fittings

- Small electric pump

- Inflatable dinghy repair kit

- Bicycle tire repair kit

- Sewing kit with variety of colored thread, needles and thimbles
- Gun cleaning/oiling kit
- Utility knife with extra blades
- Candles
- Vacuum cleaner
- Five thermometers: medical, wall mount, refrigerator, seawater, and bread
- Lots of rags
- Old toothbrushes
- Lots of clothespins

Store metal tools in dry lockers, perhaps in heavy-duty plastic boxes. Spray them with light oil to preserve and protect.

Chemicals

Ever since mariners progressed from the dugout canoe, they have employed a host of ever-improving sealants, lubricants, glues, and goops to maintain their vessels. The international voyager will do well to stock up on plenty of these items, since some may not be available in any but the most modern ports. I carry many of the following chemicals, a list you'll want to modify to suit your needs:

List of Chemicals, etc.

- Motor oil. Enough for several engine oil changes
- Transmission fluid
- Epoxy glue (5-minute and slow drying). Very strong all-purpose glue

- Underwater epoxy. Sets up in or out of the water

- White wood glue. For light mending

- Contact cement. Glue for quick repairs

- JB Weld or Marine-Tex. Metallic glue and filler

- Polyester resin and catalyst for fiberglass repairs

- Plenty of fiberglass mat, cloth, and woven roving

- Color-matched gel coat and catalyst. For cosmetic hull repairs

- WD-40 or CRC. Multi-purpose light oil preserves, lubricates, and unseizes

- Liquid wrench. Frees up corroded fasteners and parts

- Never-Seez. Anti-seize and lubricating compound

- Loctite. Bolt thread locker, prevents nuts vibrating loose

- Lubriplate multi-purpose Marine Lube 'A' grease

- Thompson's Water Seal. Waterproofs awnings, dodgers, etc.

- Water pump grease

- Teflon grease. Water resistant all purpose lubricant

- Silicone rubber sealant. General sealant

- Boat Life caulking. Marine quality caulking/bedding compound

- 5200. Very strong (permanent) adhesive bedding compound

- 3M 101. A less adhesive bedding compound for general repair

- Gasket and joint sealing compound. For plumbing and engine

- Diesel fuel treatment, alcohol-free

- Phosphoric acid, such as Ospho or Chemprime. Rusty metal treatment and rust stain remover

- Mineral spirits. Paint thinner and solvent
- Lacquer thinner. Solvent
- Acetone. Solvent
- Denatured alcohol. Solvent
- Chlorine bleach
- Rubbing compound
- Hull wax
- Paints. Including anti-fouling
- Penetrol. Paint thinner
- Clear polyurethane. Hard sealant
- Varnish
- Wood oil
- Assorted household detergents, cleaners, etc.
- Roach tablets. Very effective roach poison
- Aerosol roach bombs. Hard to find overseas
- Fly Spray and Mosquito coils
- Avon Skin-So-Soft. Gnat repellent
- Ecover brand liquid detergent. Lathers in seawater
- Comet or Ajax abrasive cleanser
- Soft Scrub non-abrasive cleanser

Spare Parts

According to writer and cruising sailor Ray Jason, "any part you have you won't need, and any part you need you won't have."

The spare parts you carry aboard will be limited by weight, space, and budget. You'll want to give first priority to those spares that may contribute to the safety of the vessel, those that will enable you to make port no matter what happens at sea. Second priority spares are those not likely to be available in any but the most modern ports. Last come non-essential, normally easy to buy spares that you might want to have available in remote places. Since every boat's equipment, storage capacity, and cruising plans are different, this list is just a starting point from which you may make your own.

Bosun's Spares

- Sail slides (cars) and hanks
- Line, enough for one complete set of running rigging, such as 300 feet of 5/8" diameter (or whatever line is common aboard), 300 feet of 1/2" diameter
- Plenty of assorted small stuff (lashing lines)
- Rigging wire, at least one piece equal in length to the longest stay aboard
- Wire terminals such as Sta-Lok
- Turnbuckles, 2 or more
- Toggles, padeyes, assorted shackles, thimbles
- Assorted blocks
- Hull repair material: fiberglass mat and cloth, resin and catalyst. (For steel hulls, welding rods and plate; for cement hulls, approved cement; for wood hulls, planking timber)
- Vast assortment of stainless steel screws (including self-tapping screws), bolts, nuts, washers, cotter pins, and clevis pins
- Assorted nails: bronze and/or stainless steel boat nails, and 1 lb. of 8-penny galvanized nails

- Male and female garden hose replacement ends
- Wicks, globes, and burners for all oil lamps
- Stern gland packing
- Oars and oarlocks for the dinghy
- Most items on the List of Chemicals

Jury Rigging Spares and Materials

- Free cutting brass: flat, bar, rod, and square stock
- Aluminum: angle, flat stock, pipe (up to 1 1/2" x the length of a spreader)
- Copper tubing and pipe
- Soft stainless steel or monel seizing wire and stainless steel trolling wire
- Duct tape
- Masking tape
- Shock cord and hook ends
- Inner tubing
- Nylon webbing
- Split connecting chain links
- Cable clamps
- Scrap wood: 2 x 4's, assorted plywood, plugs, blocks, etc.
- Scrap linoleum: 1/8" or 3/16"

Machinery Spares
(for all engines and generators)

- Zinc pencils for heat exchangers, 10

- Seawater pump impellers and seals, 4 sets

- V-belts and fan belts, 2 full sets

- Oil and fuel filters, a year's supply

- Alternator and voltage regulator, complete spare set

- Starter motor for main engine, oiled and sealed

- Starter motor brushes and a spare starter motor relay

- Hoses to repair/replace any aboard (fresh water, salt water, exhaust, oil, fuel, stuffing box and hydraulics systems)

- Assorted stainless steel hose clamps

- Solenoid

- Fuel pump repair kit

- Gaskets for heads, manifolds, pump bodies, etc., complete sets

- Gasket material, rubber and paper

- Piping, fittings, tubing

- Thermostat

- Fuel injectors, at least one, preferably a full set, packed in grease to prevent rusting

- Injector feed lines

- Water temperature and oil pressure gauges

- Ignition switches

- All specially fitted zincs (shaft, prop, hull), several of each

- Zinc fish plate
- Cutless bearing
- Propeller and prop shaft
- Stuffing box flax packing material
- Steering cables
- Repair kits for all heads, several kits
- Repair kits for every hand and foot pump aboard
- Bilge pump handle
- Rebuild kit for windvane
- Windvane vanes, 3
- Seacocks and valves
- Outboard motor parts (see manual for items)
- Water maker filters
- Water purifier replacement filters
- Tools, blades, bits. all replaceable items on tool kit list

Electrical and Electronics Spares

- GPS
- Autopilot
- Hydrometer
- Volt meter and ammeter
- Voltage regulator(s)
- Transistors for autopilot, chargers, radiotelephone, RDF
- Numerous fuses and circuit breakers for everything aboard

- Wire and terminal devices for all uses, including batteries
- Diodes for alternators, chargers, and radiotelephones
- Light bulbs for every interior and exterior light aboard (including compass, navigation lights, strobes, flashlights, dome lights, instrument lights, etc.)
- Running light lenses
- Various toggle switches and breakers
- Windlass foot switch
- Battery master switch
- Oil pressure switch
- Electrical tape
- Assorted small batteries, D-cell, C-cell, AA, AAA, etc., 1 carton
- 6-volt handheld spotlight
- 6-volt batteries for spotlight
- Refrigerator switch and Freon charging kit
- Brushes and bearings for all electric motors, (wind) generators, alternators
- VHF antenna
- Complete spare autopilot or complete autopilot parts
- Flashlights

Deck Spares

- Navigation compass
- Winch handles, 2

- Boat hook (or pole end fitting to make a boat hook)
- Running lights (kerosene or battery-powered)

Necessary Equipment Spares

- Sextant (plastic is OK for spare)
- Binoculars
- Parallel rules, dividers
- Compass (handheld compass is OK as a back-up)

Personal Spares

- Medication, especially prescription
- Prescription glasses, contact lenses
- Sunglasses, UV/polarized
- Sun protection and chap sticks
- Stationery, pens, pencils, scotch tape, paper glue, staples, rubber bands
- Camera film
- Toiletries
- Butane lighters
- Insect repellent and mosquito coil
- Rubber slings and spear heads for spear gun or sling

Chapter 16

Medicine

Medical Kit

The cruising sailor's medical kit needs to contain much more than the common first aid kit of Band-Aids, tweezers, and antibacterial cream. You can certainly assemble a medical kit for yourself, but consult your physician for advice and for any prescription items needed.

There are several pre-packed cruising medical kits on the market. One of them, the Trans-Ocean Pak, packaged by the Medical Sea Pak Company includes the following items:

- Adhesive tape, 1" (2)

- Air splints (3), foot and ankle, wrist, full arm

- Alcohol prep pads (5)

- Antacid tablets (50)

- Aspirin (100)

- Bandages, finger tip (10), knuckle (10), strip, 1"x 3" (10), strip 3/4"x 3" (50)

- Benzoin swabs (6)

- Blood pressure cuff (1)

- Bulky roll gauze 4" (2)

- Burn spray (1)

- BZK antiseptic towelettes (20)

- Calamine lotion (1);

- Cold pack, large (3), small (1)

- Cotton swabs (100)

- CPR mask and one way valve (1)

- Disposable razor (1)

- Dressing pads, 5"x 9" (5)

- Elastic bandage, 2" (3), 4" (3), 6" (4)

- Emergency blanket (1)

- Emergency dental kit (1)

- Eye pads (4)

- Eye wash (1)

- Foley catheter introduction kit (1)

- Forceps with magnifier (1)

- Gauze pads, 2" x 2" (50), 3" x 3" (24), 4" x 4" (50), 4" x 4", Extra Absorbent (12)

- Hydrogen peroxide, bottle (1)

- Ice bags (2)

- Insect bite relief swabs (5)

- Instant hot compresses (4)

- Isopropyl alcohol gel, 4 oz. (1)

- Merthiolate spray (1)
- Oil emulsion dressing (4), packs (6)
- Oral airways (3)
- Peptic relief tablets (24)
- Petroleum base ointment (1)
- Poison antidote kit (1)
- Povidone iodine, 4 oz. (1), Povidone iodine swabs (20)
- Rescue blanket, foil, heat reflective (1)
- Roll gauze, 2" (4), 4" (2), 4" sterile (10)
- Safety pins (6)
- Scalpel (1)
- Scissors, heavy bandage (1)
- Scrub sponges with antiseptic (2)
- Seizure bite stick (1)
- Skin staple remover (1)
- Skin stapler with 15 staples (2), disposable, 5 staples (1)
- Stethoscope (1)
- Splint, 1"x 6" finger (5)
- Splint, all purpose, plastic, 18" (1)
- Splint, full leg air (1)
- Surgical suture kit (2)
- Thermometer, hypothermia (low range) (1)
- Thermometer, unbreakable (1)
- Transparent covers, large (4), small (2)

- Triangle sling (1)

- Wound closure strips 1/4" (3 packs, 5 each).

Invest in one or more of the following books to keep aboard for medical treatment information: *The World Health Organization International Medical Guide for Ships* (newest edition) *Advanced First Aid Afloat* by Peter F. Eastman, M.D., *The Cruising Sailor's Medical Guide* by Nicholas C. Leone, M.D., *First Aid Afloat* by Paul B. Sheldon, M.D., or *Your Offshore Doctor* by Michael Beilan, M.D. No doubt there are other excellent medical books available.

All crewmembers should be CPR qualified. There are courses readily available to learn this basic, life-saving technique. In addition, training in the following skills could prove invaluable: first aid including cardiopulmonary resuscitation, applying simple strapping and plaster casts, skin suturing, inserting intravenous cannulae and giving intravenous fluids, giving both intramuscular and intravenous injections, endotracheal intubation and cricothyrotomy, and applying temporary dental fillings.

Vitamins are a form of preventive medicine, and vitamin deficiency is a potential threat when cruising in remote regions where fresh supplies are scarce. Stock up on plenty of Vitamin C and a good multi-vitamin, at least. Better still, read some books on natural health or visit a health food store or a holistic nutritionist to seek more information on vitamin supplements and good nutrition. To fully enjoy the cruising life, you need to maintain your body at least as well as you maintain your boat.

Remember: Use a powerful UV sun block cream daily when cruising, and wear a hat or sun visor. If you spend a lot of time in the sun as many sailors do, visit a dermatologist periodically for a check-up.

Chapter 17

ⵞ

Miscellaneous Gear

Foul-Weather Gear

Invest in basic, high quality, heavy duty, yellow colored (not white or blue, which can't be easily seen in the water), totally waterproof rain gear for captain and crew. Include sea boots, the ones commercial fishermen wear being less stylish but perhaps more waterproof and definitely less expensive than the marine boutique variety. Strong safety harnesses (with 6-foot tethers and stainless steel carabiner clips) for everyone aboard are an absolute must. Attach a brass or heavy-duty plastic whistle and a waterproof light (or strobe light) to each harness. Each person should have one or more pencil flares and a sharp rigging knife in the pockets of their foul-weather gear.

Some foul-weather suits feature positive flotation, and a built-in safety harness. In addition, there are a variety of survival suits available. They provide waterproof warmth on deck, and can keep you afloat and alive for a long time in the water, preventing hypothermia with their excellent insulation. Foul-weather gear is evolving and improving. Check out the latest features in catalogs and at boat shows.

Fishing Gear

Most cruising sailors care enough about the ocean not to kill its occupants unnecessarily in the name of sport. I fish only for food, using a hand spool, heavy fishing line and stainless steel leader, along with a variety of trolling lures. Of course, many sailors use a rod and reel, fishing the harbors and reefs they visit. The real experts catch baitfish with a throw-net, which requires a technique I've almost but never quite mastered. In the tropics I prefer to simply dive in and spear fish with a Hawaiian sling. Some cruisers carry fish, lobster and/or crab traps, baiting and lowering them over the side when anchored. Plan to avail yourself of the sea's bounty but, please, don't abuse it.

Be aware that ciguatera poisoning from eating certain fish is a definite hazard in many subtropical regions, including the West Indies. More than 1,000,000 cases of ciguatera occur annually worldwide, especially in areas around Puerto Rico, Hawaii, Australia, Indonesia and Micronesia. According to at least one researcher, "a map of the tropics is a map of ciguatera." Ask local fishermen which fish are safe to eat and which ones are not.

Dive Gear

In addition to recreational use, a mask-fins-and-snorkel set is necessary for underwater chores: Cleaning the bottom, checking an anchor set and untangling a line from the propeller are all-too-common uses. If you have the space, scuba gear adds another dimension to water sports as well as increased capability to accomplish submarine tasks. Build in secure air tank storage racks if you carry this equipment aboard your boat. There are compact air compressors on the market for refilling tanks aboard.

I did not carry tanks aboard my last boat, but did bring my own BC, regulator, weight belt and light wetsuit. Not only was I able to rent tanks reasonably in most of the areas where I wanted to scuba dive, but more than once I was able to rent them right there on the reef, from dive boats that came out with tourist divers.

Cameras

The cruising life offers unique opportunities for photography. You'll find yourself using zoom or telephoto lenses more than you did ashore because subjects are often some distance away from the boat.

Regardless of whether you bring other cameras and equipment, consider buying a small waterproof camera. There are a variety of compact waterproof 35mms on the market. This not only opens up the possibility of underwater photography to you, but is also safer on deck, in the dinghy and on hikes.

Bicycles

Bicycles enhance the cruise life, providing mobility ashore to explore and run errands. Folding bikes are easy to store and to carry ashore in the dinghy. I cruised for years with a pair of stainless steel 3-speeds made in Taiwan for Dahon of California. What they lacked in performance (due to their small wheel size), they made up for in stowability on the boat. Each folded up in a minute to the size of a large suitcase; the pair stowed in one deep locker under a settee. Dahon also makes a folding bike with a larger (21") wheel size, and a folding mountain bike that isn't marinized.

There are other, full-size folding and non-folding bikes on the market that would increase the range and variety of cycling exploration ashore. I've discovered mountain biking since my last long sailing cruise. Next time I go cruising, I'm bringing a full-size mountain bike along, even if I have to partially disassemble it by removing the wheels and handlebars to store it on board. Of course, all ferrous metal parts need to be greased, oiled or painted regularly to prevent them from rusting.

Seair Dynamics of Jupiter, Florida builds well-engineered, lightweight folding bicycle trailers that are terrific for hauling groceries, equipment and small children to and from the boat.

More Stuff

Lots of cruisers have pets aboard. However, some countries restrict their entry. Check with the embassies or consulates before you go.

When you're cruising, it isn't always possible to take pets ashore. Give some thought to how your pet will cope with that. Most cats, and many dogs, will use a kitty litter box when they're stuck on the boat. Another trick is to train your pet to go on a piece of Astroturf on the aft deck (the poop deck?). If you've tied a piece of line to this, it's easy to toss it overboard for a rinse.

As with small children, lifeline netting will help keep pets from falling overboard. A safety harness for dogs is also a good idea. Off-shore, the harness can be tethered to a central point above the cockpit, allowing some freedom of movement while insuring the animal's safety. Belowdecks, carpet or throw rugs protect the cabin sole's finish from being scratched by claws while providing a better grip for them.

If possible, provide a way for pets to pass freely between the cockpit and the cabin. Not all animals can use a companionway ladder. In Spain, I adopted a small mutt, La Rosa Española de Sevilla, who then cruised with me for years. Rosa could enter and exit the cabin through an opening porthole between the quarter berth and the cockpit (see Figure 22).

Figure 22: SPARROW's canine crew, Rosa, let herself in and out through the quarter-berth porthole.

She added so much to the pleasure of my cruising and my life that I never considered it a burden having her along.

There's no end to the paraphernalia you can buy for a cruising sailboat. New products and improved versions of standard gear are appearing all the time, especially in the electronics field. Browsing through a large boat show is one of the best ways to keep abreast of new developments in marine equipment, but as I've mentioned before, boating publications, Internet chat groups and bulletin boards, and the scuttlebutt on the docks can all be valuable sources of up-to-the-minute information.

Chapter 18

⌒

Documents and Officialdom

One potential snag in paradise is dealing with the regulations and representatives of the various governments whose countries we visit. Each time we clear in or clear out, we must learn and comply with a new set of rules and paperwork. Customs, Immigration, the Port Captain, the National Guard, the Army, the Navy, and All the King's Men want forms completed in triplicate, signatures, stamps, fees and taxes and above all, respect. I have met many truly pleasant officials who, when approached with a friendly greeting and a respectful attitude, are polite, everyday people content with a secure, low-paying and often dull job. But there are a few out there—small men in big uniforms—who will dislike (or resent or envy) you for your apparent wealth, your skin color, your nationality, your boat, or whatever. They can make a sailor's life miserable in a hundred tedious ways. We must do our best to mollify them by presenting all ship's papers in proper order, along with a diplomatic (if not humble) demeanor.

Important Papers List

Always carry the following aboard your boat:

- Ship's log recording, at least, dates and times of departures and arrivals from port to port, weather observations underway, and notable events occurring aboard or pertaining to your vessel (I use a thick, lined, hardcover Records book purchased at an office supply store.)

- Ship's registration or official document proving ownership

- Notarized letter of authorization permitting you to be operating the vessel if you are not the owner of record (or if the boat is registered to a corporation)

- Valid passports for everyone aboard

- Visas, obtained in advance for those countries that require visitors to obtain visas prior to arrival

- International immunization certificates for everyone aboard, showing up-to-date inoculations for countries that require it

- Crew list, listing each person's name, address, passport number, and position aboard (captain, crew or passenger). If your crew remains the same during the cruise, make up copies in advance to hand over to, and sign in front of, the official requiring it in each port

- Official clearance from your last port of call when available and/or required

- List of all firearms aboard stating make, model, serial number, and the exact amount of ammunition for each gun

- Proof of financial solvency for countries that require it, such as a bank statement, or cash, or traveler's checks

- International health and vaccination certificates for any pets aboard, and in some cases, prior written permission from the host country's consulate for the pet to visit

- Cruising permit and all other required forms of the host country, issued by them during the entry procedure and retained by you afterwards

- Ship's VHF radio call sign and station license, obtained in the United States from the FCC in Gettysburg, Pennsylvania

- SSB and/or ham radio licenses, if you have that equipment

- List of your native country's embassies and consulates around the world, and those of each crewmember of a different nationality, including addresses and phone numbers.

Note: Make photocopies of all your important papers, including passports, ship's documents, etc. Keep one set of copies aboard, wrapped in plastic and stored in the survival kit, or at least stored separately from the originals. Leave another set with a friend, relative, or agent in case you need them forwarded quickly. You can't imagine the hassle this will save if the original documents are ever lost or stolen.

One other thing. The postal systems of some third world countries range from slow to impossible. It's a good idea to carry a supply of U.S. postage stamps aboard. You can often find a sympathetic, homeward-bound tourist, or a fellow cruiser flying back for a visit, who is willing to take your mail to post stateside. However, it is unfair to ask a stranger or a casual acquaintance to carry back a package for you because airlines and customs officers would hold them responsible for its contents.

Chapter 19

⌒⌒

The Bare Essentials

I've discussed quite a few items that can go aboard a sailboat to trick her out for world cruising. Most of what I've suggested is useful; some is necessary. Only you, the captain, can make the final determination regarding what you'll carry on your own vessel. Some mariners have crossed oceans in kayaks and papyrus reed rafts, while others have perished at sea in great ships equipped with every modern convenience. It doesn't matter so much what you've got as how you use what you've got.

What I'm getting at is that you can go cruising without most of the stuff listed in this book. My aim has been to make you aware of the possibilities, not to frighten you off with the sheer volume and expense of it all. The most important thing to bring aboard any boat is the right mental attitude. An optimistic, positive approach to your task will accomplish wonders when applied to outfitting the modern cruising sailboat, as it will in all other aspects of life. A burning desire to go cruising is the primary ingredient that will power you through the obstacles, and overcome shortcomings in equipment and budget. What comprises the *bare essentials* for cruising depends on the style of the people who are going, and on the climate and characteristics of the region(s) to be visited. Let's take a look at what you really, really, absolutely have to have:

- You need a boat that floats, a means of propelling it, food and fresh water, and an adventurous spirit.

That's the end of Bare Essentials List #1.

Now we can add on forever, according to our own wants and needs. But let's keep it relatively simple and inexpensive:

- Proof of boat ownership

- Vessel registration or documentation, especially if there's an engine in the boat

- If you're visiting another country, a valid passport. (Note: some countries in the Western Hemisphere will accept an American's birth certificate and/or voter registration card as proof of citizenship)

- At least in U.S. waters, the Coast Guard required life jackets, horn, flares, fire extinguisher(s), etc.

- Compass

- Running lights

- A rain suit, or at least a waterproof poncho

- Basic tool kit: at least a sharp knife, pliers, screwdrivers, wrenches, hammer, etc.

- If you're going offshore, a sextant, an accurate time piece, and the necessary tables for celestial navigation

- Charts, dividers, parallel ruler, pencils, paper

- Regional cruising guide book

- Radar reflector

- Binoculars

- Flashlight and batteries

- Bilge pump(s)

- Dinghy with oars

- A couple of good anchors with rode and chain

- System for reefing sails

- Sail covers

- Sail repair kit

- Rain catcher

- Water storage tanks or containers

- Cockpit shade awning or bimini top (in the tropics)

- Survival kit and something to get into if your boat sinks or burns, if only a dinghy

- Radio receiver for weather reports, even if it's just a portable AM radio

- Some form of self-steering (a home-made windvane can work fine and it's cheap to build)

- Dock lines and lashing lines

- A couple of fenders (even if they're old car tires)

- Bucket and deck brush

- If there's an engine, some basic maintenance materials such as oil, transmission fluid, and a manual. And fuel.

- If there's an electrical system aboard, a multi-meter tester, some wire, and distilled water for any lead-acid batteries

- Stove, stove fuel, pots, pans, eating and cooking utensils

- Food

- Handheld spotlight (6-volt is fine, with batteries)

- A lead line for sounding depths

- Flags for foreign travel: quarantine flag, courtesy flag, and your national ensign

- Long water hose

- Sunglasses, UV/polarized

- Duct tape

- Epoxy glue and silicone seal

- Ecover brand liquid soap

- Ship's helicopter (just kidding!)

Have I forgotten anything?

Afterword

I think most of us go cruising to find the freedom, the adventure, and the spirit of life lacking in our modern society. We travel to remote harbors to live simpler lifestyles, closer to nature and to ourselves. We go for the people we meet, for the places we experience, and for the stories we can tell. Most of all, we go to have fun.

Cruising under sail is a school in which we're learning how to live in harmony with our world, and how to enjoy it. Outfitting the boat is the entrance exam into that school. Or maybe it's actually the first course in a long and rewarding curriculum. Either way, it seems that the more we learn, the more we realize there is to learn.

Toward that end, I would appreciate your input on this book. If you have discovered a piece of equipment or a system that particularly enhances your cruising sailboat or cruising life, something I've overlooked or misrepresented in this book, please share it with me along with any other errors or omissions you discover in these pages. If/when I revise the text for future printings, I'd like to include your ideas. E-mail me at ready@tor.cc

I wish you great voyaging. Plan ahead. Have fun.
Reef Early!

Sparrow's Specifications

Pacific Seacraft Crealock 37

LOA	36'11"
LWL	27'9"
Beam	10'10"
Design draft (Scheel keel)	4'6"
Actual (loaded) cruising draft	5'0"
Mast clearance	47'6"
Design displacement	16,000 lbs
Estimated cruising displacement	20,000 lbs
External lead ballast	6,200 lbs
Cutter rig sail area	758 sq. ft.
Auxiliary engine	44-hp Yanmar 4-cyl. Diesel
Fuel tank	40 U.S. gallons
Water tanks	90 U.S. gallons
Hull	Fiberglass
Spars	Aluminum
Designer	W.I.B. Crealock
Builder	Pacific Seacraft Corp. Fullerton, CA

Index

About the Author

Tor Pinney is a cruising sailor and writer. He has logged nearly 150,000 nautical miles as a professional offshore delivery captain and charter skipper, and as the owner of five different liveaboard sailboats. He holds a United States Coast Guard Merchant Marine Officer Master's License.

Tor sold SPARROW after sailing her more than 30,000 miles during a six-year cruise. As of this printing, he is president of Anchor Yacht Sales (www.AnchorYachts.com), dealer for American-built Valiant Yachts cruising sailboats, distributor for Nova Scotia-built Cape Island Trawlers, and broker for pre-owned cruising sailboats and trawlers of every kind. Anchor Yacht Sales is based in Barrington, Rhode Island. Tor's next extended cruise will likely be to the South Pacific, Southeast Asia and East Africa.

Tor's sea stories and articles appear regularly in American boating magazines such as *Cruising World, Sail,* and *Yachting,* and in numerous publications abroad. Many of these articles are posted on the Internet at www.tor.cc